Becoming A Lion

WRITTEN & ILLUSTRATED
BY LIZ MANNCHEN

PEGASUS PAPERBACK

© Copyright 2025
Liz Mannchen

The right of Liz Mannchen to be identified as author of this
work has been asserted by her in accordance with the
Copyright, Designs and Patents Act 1988

All Rights Reserved

No reproduction, copy or transmission of this publication
may be made without written permission.
No paragraph of this publication may be reproduced,
copied or transmitted save with the written permission of the publisher, or in
accordance with the provisions of the Copyright Act 1956 (as amended).

Any person who does any unauthorised act in relation to
this publication may be liable to criminal
prosecution and civil claims for damage.

A CIP catalogue record for this title is
available from the British Library

ISBN 978 1 80016 033 9

Pegasus is an imprint of
Pegasus Elliot MacKenzie Publishers Ltd.
www.pegasuspublishers.com

First Published in 2025

Pegasus
Sheraton House Castle Park
Cambridge CB3 0AX England

Printed & Bound in Great Britain

DEDICATION

This book is dedicated to all my fears that, like bats, have invited me throughout my life to explore the deepest and darkest caves to find these hidden treasures. To every adversity and challenge I've ever faced, that taught me not to lie down like an opossum but face them dead on.

To my wolf, Ulrich, whose love has empowered me to live wild and free, may we never stop chasing our dreams. To my Bo Bei, who wears her tortoise shell like a lion's mane, may you grow up to be more fierce than your mother. To the Golin and Mannchen pack, may you continue to brave your journeys.

To my mother, who always pushed me to find my light, may you never lose yours. To my father, may you finally rest in peace like a moth on the moon. And to my Heavenly Father, the one true lion, may this book reveal more of your wild, fierce, and brave love for us all.

ACKNOWLEDGEMENTS

Three people empowered me to make this book possible. Ulrich Mannchen, thank you for all the long walks in the woods where we dreamed and developed these characters. Thank you for believing I could do this and allowing me time and space to lock myself in our basement and release all these treasures out of the cave in my mind and onto paper. Matthew McCaigue, thank you for your beautiful graphic design. And to Anna Mosena, who took a risk on this dyslexic who dreamed of writing a book. Your edits and support made this book eminently more readable than it otherwise might have been. Without you all, this book would not exist. Thank you.

Pegasus Elliot Mackenzie Publishers, thank you for believing in this book and giving it life!

This is a work of fiction. Names, characters, businesses, places, events and incidents are either the product of the author's imagination or used in a fictitious manner. Any resemblance to actual persons, living or dead, or actual events is purely coincidental.

INTRO

I am not a lion. Lions are strong and brave, and walk in a posture of courage and might. I am a broken, flawed, and painfully insecure person. I am swimming in a world of monsters and beasts that daily challenge my character and demand I examine my integrity. And more often than not, I fail to rise up and be anything remotely resembling a strong, brave lion. The claws that I so desperately want to sharpen with might and bravery are dulled down by caution and anxiety. The posture of pride is shadowed by shame. The roar that should sound out freedom and justice is often strangled into a whisper of apathy and passivity. I am not a lion. But I want to be a lion.

I believe that everyone is born with a lion inside them, daring to be set free. Daily, we choose to cage or unleash that beast through the choices we make when faced with adversity and hardship. I believe that no matter how hard, painful, and hopeless life can seem, there is enough courage and bravery inside us all, and inside the strong community of lions around us, to overcome and face it. And I, for one, want to spend the rest of my life trying to become that lion, surrounding myself with lions and helping others become lions.

I have met many beasts and creatures on my journey that have shaped me into becoming a lion: friends, foes, challenges and situations in my life that I have characterized into different animals that I have learned from. Bats, tortoises, wolves, possums and a few too many moths, through their own characteristics and behaviors, have taught me about being a lion. Facing fears, surviving hard seasons of life, knowing when to back down and when to fight, and identifying unhealthy areas of my life and relationships are a few things these beasts have taught me. As we journey through this book, may these animals help you, too, become a lion.

CONTENTS

BATS
- BATS TURNED VAMPIRES 11
- TREASURES OF THE CAVE 16
- THINGS I'VE LEARNED FROM BATS 23

WOLVES
- LONE WOLVES 25
- I MARRIED A WOLF 33
- THINGS I'VE LEARNED FROM WOLVES 43

TORTOISES
- CHIPPED SHELLS 45
- COMFORT SHELL 52
- THINGS I'VE LEARNED FROM TORTOISES 66

POSSUMS
- POSSUMING OUT 69
- PEACEMAKERS VS PEACE LOVERS 79
- THINGS I'VE LEARNED FROM POSSUMS 89

MOTHS
- MOTH INFESTATION 91
- THE PURSUIT OF LIGHT 104
- THINGS I'VE LEARNED FROM MOTHS 113

LIONS
- BECOMING A LION 115
- EPILOGUE 122
- ABOUT THE AUTHOR 124

BATS TURNED VAMPIRES

Did you know that bats are the only mammals that truly fly? And while it sounds crazy, they make up a whopping twenty percent of the population of all mammal species on Earth. They also have life spans that can reach up to three and a half times longer than other mammals the same size, some up to thirty years. They feed on fruits and small insects, and some species can eat over one thousand insects in one hour.

When I was nine months old, my mother walked into the living room and found me playing with a baby bat. Apparently, it had made its way down from the attic, noticed an intrigued and curious child, and decided that I was good company. My mother, curiously, did not share the same sentiment and promptly flipped out. I believe it was during this encounter that my lifelong fascination with bats began. A few Halloweens later, as we celebrated what would become my favorite holiday, I found a rubber toy bat and completely fell in love with it. I lugged him all over the place and fed him hot dogs. Yeah, I was a weird kid.

Sadly, my fascination took a dark turn when I was around ten years old. I slept over at a friend's house, and as usual, struggled to fall asleep in a home other than my own. Normally, I would wait for everyone to fall asleep and then I would call my parents to come pick me up. But on this occasion, I hatched a plan to stay up all night and proudly announce that I hadn't slept a wink. I would be just like a bat! As I lay there, wide awake, my friend annoyingly slept like an angel beside me. Then, hearing the TV

in another room, I realized that her older brother and his friends were watching a movie. I curiously tiptoed into the room to join them, and there on the screen I saw the monster that would forever change my innocent fascination with bats: a vampire. I stood there white as a ghost, shivering with fear as this bat-like human's white fangs, dripping in blood, sank into the neck of the victim he meant to devour. To be fair, it was Leslie Nielsen starring in 'Dracula: Dead and Loving It'. But I was only ten, and I was horrified. At that very moment, my lifelong (and irrational, I suppose) fear of vampires began.

Soon after, I learned about vampire bats and their dietary intake of blood, and the connection between this innocent animal and the fictitious monster seemed plausible. Thus, my love for bats slowly became entangled with my fear of vampires. To this day, I still deal with an intense fear of vampires. I am easily startled when anyone breathes on my neck. I experience a shiver of fear and will often scream or cry. My poor husband has borne his share of absurdly strong reactions after merely giving me a hug and exhaling while doing so. I mean goodness, just inhale and hold it, please. Unsurprisingly, turtlenecks became my friends.

As I grew older and tried to deal with this ridiculous phobia I have of an imaginary creature, I realized that vampires are a lot like my fears. Often they are things I initially loved, like bats, that have been manipulated, exploited, or corrupted. Something that was once pure was turned into something terrifying. Fears, like vampires, prey on the weak and insecure. They hide out in the dark crevices of our minds and wait for the lies that echo around us to tell us exactly when and where to attack.

Once they've attacked, they feed, and when they feed, they grow, and if they grow, they multiply, forming more and more lies and fears inside our heads to the point where they are flying around so quickly and fiercely that we no longer remember what is real and what is not. What is a bat, and what is a vampire? I know that vampires are not real. I also know that bats are not vicious creatures, just like I know that half the fears I allow to live, dwell in and control my mind and life are also not real. But the way they make me feel, and prompt such strong emotions, is entirely real. Those are not lies. And if we don't deal with our fears, much like bats, they can live on for decades.

So how do we turn vampires back into bats? We must be brave enough to look deep into the crevices and caves in our minds, summon the courage of a lion, and face our vampire fears. When we look those blood-sucking beasts in the eye, we might find things we did not expect to uncover. People we fear are often ones we love or once loved. Dreams we once chased are now dreaded, because a person or circumstance told us they were unattainable. We deny opportunities because the chance of failure is too terrifying to compete with our longing to succeed. And we reject truth because the lies are more comfortable to believe.

But what if we could reverse our fears, taking warning signs and turn them into invitations? What if the anxiety and the nerves we feel around certain people, conversations, or opportunities could shift from a signal to run and escape to an invitation that prompts us to explore the possibilities and desires concealed behind those feelings? What if facing our vampires could lead us back to our bats? What if facing our fears could lead to more than just freedom, even to unveiled treasures? What if we could get back to feeding our bats hotdogs, rather than our peace of mind?

TREASURES OF THE CAVE

Because most bats are nocturnal, they fly and hunt for their food at night. And since they sleep during the day, bats seek dark, protected shelters like caves for refuge and a home. In order to stay out of reach of enemies, bats hang from the ceilings of caves and often live in large colonies, some up to twenty million bats! Also, contrary to popular belief, bats are not blind. Their eyes are tuned to low-light conditions, which are enhanced by other senses, such as hearing. With a remarkably evolved sense of hearing, bats bounce sounds off objects along their path, transferring echoes to fellow bats. This allows them to identify their prey in the darkness.

Whether you have crawled, fallen into, been banished to, or actively chosen to enter a new season of life, you are entering the unknown. You step into worlds that are unfamiliar and paths that are unrevealed and obscure. And in this unrecognizable and unknown place, it can oftentimes feel dark, lonely and even scary, much like a mysterious cave.

During those transitions into many new, different seasons of life, I have often found myself feeling alone, as if lost in a cave. Whether it was beginning a new relationship, starting a new job, moving to a new country, getting married or entering into motherhood, the new, unfamiliar season ahead of me has often felt like trying to navigate a mysterious cavern in the exploration of treasures. And with no map to navigate me through, it has always forced me to learn new skills and adapt to my new reality.

Some seasons began smoothly with the choice and excitement of diving in, while others began with fright, born out of unwanted and unplanned circumstances. Whatever the situation that leads you to a new cave, I find that these new seasons come with the uncertainty of what is to come and the loss of what is behind. In these moments, such a journey is often accompanied by a significant confrontation of fear. This fear can either break you, or it can establish you, shaping who you will become and what you will find in this season of your cave.

These new phases in our lives also come with a certain amount of curiosity as well as fear. The pursuit of treasures we might find hidden in the unknown can pull us forward, while the uncertainty of risk can push us away. The excitement of getting to know someone pulls us closer into the cave of a new relationship, while the fear of how we might get hurt pushes us back to the entrance. Like entering an actual cave, we begin

our journey through a passageway that is still connected to the world we know — a world filled with light that allows us to see and understand what is around us and how it works. When we enter a cave and move forward in exploration, we relinquish the light, the known, in order to explore the darkness and the unknown. We let go of our right to assurance, control, and understanding in order to explore the unknown. And that can be terrifying!

Those who brave the unknown of the new season know that the farther and deeper into the cave you go, the harder it is to see. You no longer have control of what you are doing because you no longer know where you are, or where you are going, or what is about to happen. New seasons of our lives present us with obstacles and challenges we've never faced before. And in this discomfort and unknown, the fear begins to sink in.

For most, this is the moment of defeat. The darkness swallows them up with fear — not of the darkness itself, but of what the darkness masks. What, or who might we find or become, the deeper we journey into this cave? What are we leaving behind and letting go with each step forward? What might happen if I say yes to this new job, or who will I become if I enter into this marriage? The fear of the unknown can either intrigue or paralyze you. And for those that allow the fear of the unknown to overpower them, they risk either getting stuck inside, trapped in the loneliness and isolation of the dark cave, or allow it to drive them away completely, banishing them from the exploration of the cave and sending them back to familiar light.

Either way, the fear has won. It has captured you or it has overpowered you and stopped you from pursuing the treasures

ahead. When the darkness of fear swallows you up, you stop growing. You stop fighting for your dreams, or setting goals, engaging in new things and connecting to new people: you stop exploring new caves. When you refuse to enter into the unknown territories for fear of what you might find inside, you stop growing and miss out on unbelievable treasures that come only through exploration of the darkness.

But those that brave the darkness — indulging in all that the unknown brings — reap what it offers. For darkness not only offers the invitation to be brave, but also to learn, depend, adopt new skills and parts of yourself that you never would have before entering the cave. Things that will not only help you navigate through this new season, but triumph through it as you delight in its treasures.

Being nocturnal, bats have adapted to the darkness. During the night they explore, hunt and fly. During the day they live deep in the darkness of habitats like caves. Most bats use echolocation. They create rapid, high-pitched squeaks called 'ultra sounds', and listen to these sounds bounce off objects, allowing bats not only to navigate through the darkness but also hunt their prey. They have learned to use the darkness to their benefit, making it no surprise that bats are quite superior animals who are, despite their size, some of the longest-lived and most populous mammals on earth.

Like bats, we too can choose to fear the darkness or learn and benefit from it. The treasures that come from exploring seasons, people, and opportunities that are unknown to us can either cripple us with fear or grow, develop and mature us into superior versions of ourselves. I know for myself that any interesting, important or profound thing I ever did in my life came with a significant confrontation of fear of the dark and

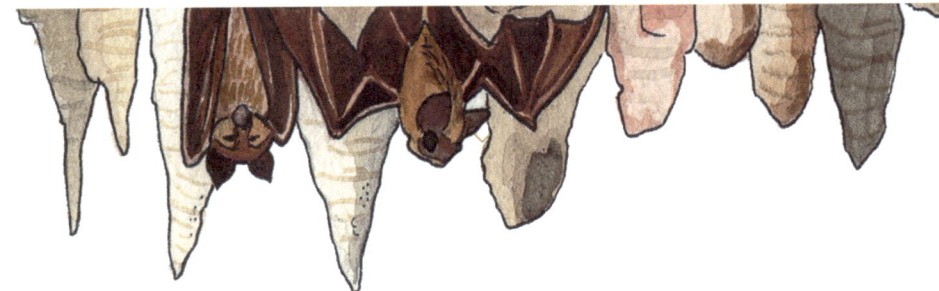

unknown. And out of the confrontation of that fear came the most incredible treasures of my life.

What is the cave you fear to enter? Maybe it's a new relationship? A new job? A new language, land or role in your life? Imagine for a second the treasures you might find in that cave if you were to pursue it and then ask yourself — are these treasures worth going through the terrifying darkness to find? And if so, trust that you too will adapt, grow, and find the strength to not only navigate your caves, but conquer your fears and turn them into some of the biggest, most incredible treasures of your life.

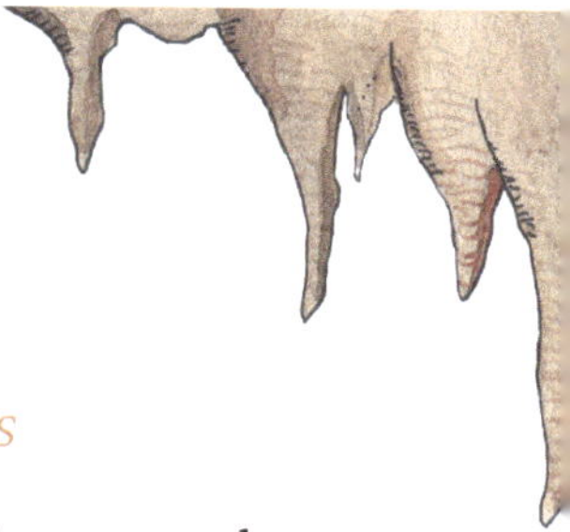

THINGS I'VE LEARNED FROM BATS

- Fears are often things we originally loved that have turned into fears. The only way to restore the things fear robbed us of is by braving the invitation to explore them.

- Oftentimes the best, most significant treasures in our lives are found on the other side of fear.

- Braving the entrance of the darkest, hardest, most uncomfortable seasons of our lives, which feel much like caves, will not only reward you with treasures only found inside the cave, but the treasures of who you become while in it.

"May the invitations your bats give you to confront your fears unleash the bravery of the lion inside you that can turn them into treasures."

LONE WOLVES

Wolves are pack animals that often stick together for life. However, fifteen percent of wolves will become 'lone wolves' that venture out on their own by choice or banishment. Abandoning the pack means leaving behind the protection other members offer, and loners must be cautious about trespassing into lands belonging to other packs. To survive, a lone wolf might need to search for hundreds of miles, conceal its whereabouts and limit its howling, which could give away its location to enemies. Without the support of a pack, lone wolves are likely to die unless they learn to fend for themselves and become strong on their own. But just because a wolf leaves its home doesn't mean it's alone forever. Many eventually return to their natal pack or find a new one to join.

At some point in our lives, we will all feel like part of a pack, and we will all feel like lone wolves. Humans are natural pack animals. We gravitate toward belonging to something bigger than ourselves. Whether it's your family, friends, work colleagues, team, religion, band, etc., we want and need to belong — to be accepted, supported and protected. We want to be seen and affirmed and valued. But in most of our lives, there will come at least one (or perhaps several) phases where we separate, are banished, pushed out, or severed from our packs, whether it be from broken families, orphanhood, being fired, losing friends, divorce, deaths, breakups, war, asylum, or other causes for splits and separations. At some point in your life, voluntarily or not, you will likely come to a point where you must strive and defend yourself on your own — a point at which you become a lone wolf.

Growing up, my family was my pack. As flawed and faulty as we were, we were a pack. I loved our pack. Because of it, I knew I belonged, and it belonged to me. I knew my place in the pack. I knew everyone's roles and how to function. And in an uncertain, volatile world, our pack of instability was my stability. And when, to my horror, our pack dismantled, so did my world. Being a child of divorce I know, as many know, when your parents separate, often the entire pack separates and everyone in the family suddenly becomes lone wolves. When my parents divorced, both my mother and father moved away. My sister and I moved to different cities for college, and soon after I packed my bags and moved halfway across the world. Over a decade later, we all continue to live in separate places and have very independent lives.

Displacement from my pack created a lasting effect of chaos and confusion in my life. Much like a lone wolf, when I left home, I found myself incredibly disoriented and confused. I felt

like a vagabond traveling the world, desperately trying to find out where and to whom I belonged.

As humans, those who live as lone wolves try to rise above dependency and the need for others. They make their way through this world on their own strengths and rules. By protecting themselves through the barriers they create, they often live lives of isolation, believing this brings freedom from the pain they once endured while enslaved to a former pack. Those who are pack seekers, on the other hand, search for this same freedom through dependency on others. They desire to be named and identify with something, and believe their value comes from the community found in a pack. They are often hoping that the sanctification of a new pack will redeem the brokenness of a former one.

After my family split, I roamed around living in various places, dating various people, going in and out of jobs and schools and making an array of poor life choices — all of which were responses to the constant need and search I was on for a new pack. After a few years of living this way, I suddenly and unexpectedly hit rock bottom. Every single area of my life unfathomably fell apart in just two weeks when a string of unrelated events occurred: I was fired, dumped, left without a place to live and unable to go to school. Crushed and lost, I did what most lone wolves do: I fled. I heard about a photography school in Germany, and within two weeks I had sold my belongings, got a passport, and jumped on a plane to a country I'd never been to before for a school I had little knowledge of or real interest in. I was escaping and leaving everything behind in the hope of finding something new ahead.

When I floundered into Germany and finally arrived at my school in a small village in the middle of nowhere in the East, I'm pretty sure I must have appeared to most everyone there like one of those deranged, unhealthy lone wolves that you wouldn't want to poke with a ten-foot pole. I was a mess. I was so disoriented and confused about where I was and where I'd just come from that my behavior and attitude was probably unrecognizable to who I truly am. Of course, this is precisely when I met my soon-to-be husband. (I will be referring to him as my 'wolf', and soon you will find out why.) And no, I'm afraid it wasn't love at first sight. I was such a mess that he wasn't sure what to do with me — I mean, I wasn't even sure what to do with me.

I barely knew where I was, surrounded by people I didn't know, in a country I'd never been to, with a language I didn't speak. No friends, no family, just me. Alone, lost and isolated in my life and my mind, much like a wandering, lonely wolf. And yet, in this season of being completely stripped of everything I knew and came from, who I thought I was and what I thought was important, I learned one of the best life lessons that comes with being a lone wolf.

When you are completely broken, the only choice you have is to stay broken or rebuild. And when nothing is left because there is nothing to lose, everything is possible.

I had a new foundation to become whoever and whatever I wanted, unattached to anything, anyone, any society, and any pack telling me what or who I needed to be. That also meant being without a pack who would support or protect me, and that became as exhilarating as it was terrifying. The more I braved the role of a lone wolf, the more I explored who I really was on my own, just as me. The more isolated I was, the more I had to face fears and conflicts on my own, making me stronger and braver. The farther I moved from the direction my old pack had been going, the more I moved in the direction my independence was leading me to, which opened up a whole new world in which to explore new goals and ideas and adventures. And the more alone I was, the more comfortable, accepting and loving I became of myself, because at that point, I was all I had.

Eventually, I became comfortable and confident being on my own. I figured out who I was and what I wanted. I knew how to survive in this world without a pack and how to thrive on my own. And eventually, I came to the inevitable fork in the road that every lone wolf will one day face: the opportunity to join a new pack.

My life had slowly moved from isolation to invitation. As I grew more comfortable with who I was, it seemed as though new doors were opening up for me to join others again. New friendships, relationships, work and social communities were forming and forcing me to decide if I wanted to open myself up again to a new season of my life — this time with others. And eventually the biggest invitation, inevitably ending my lone wolf years for good, came when my wolf asked me to marry him.

As I wandered around and explored life as a lone wolf, my wolf and I became friends. Then we started a relationship. And then we began heading towards marriage. And in that season, being in a relationship and feeling things shift toward real commitment, I was faced with a nerve-wracking question: do I really want to live as a lone wolf forever, or am I brave enough to join another pack?

The thought of joining my wolf and forming a new pack with him forced me to face my fear of belonging to something or someone again. Here was a chance to join a pack that could possibly fall apart and leave me yet again broken and alone. And this time, it would be a family I would choose and be responsible for keeping together, not just one I was born into. Was I ready for that? Was I even still made for that?

When facing my fear of this kind of commitment, I asked myself if my fear of marriage was actually a bat turned vampire. Had I once loved the idea of belonging to a pack and to others, but due to the pain that separation caused me before, had I learned to fear it? I came to the conclusion that marriage had always been a bat: something I always wanted and believed in and felt made for, but due to the unavoidable pain that came with broken marriages, relationships, and former packs in my past, I had come to fear it and what it could become.

I knew that facing my fear would hold an invitation to find new treasures - treasures I believed I was ready to find, because of the lonely yet empowering season behind me. Learning to be a lone wolf prepared me for braving the next step of joining a pack.

Through finding and refining myself, I felt confident that I would not lose myself inside a pack. I knew who I was, and would be able to define the strengths I could bring to a new unit. Through learning to love myself without anyone else, I learned how I could love a pack.

And eventually I did just that. My wolf and I married in a stretch of Bavarian forest that belonged to his family, surrounded by men in lederhosen, bratwurst and family and friends who had gathered from around the world. In a white dress of feathers, I glided down the aisle like a swan to my wolf, and we became a new pack. I remember sitting there at our wedding, looking out at all those people, all those friends from back home and all the friends I met on my journey. All the new family I was marrying into and all those family members whose packs I still belonged to, no matter how different it looked that day. I remember thinking how grateful I was for my season of being a lone wolf, and at the same time for my choice to not live that way forever. Living on your own can teach you many beautiful, wonderful things about yourself and about life. But I have come to find that those things are always more beautiful when lived amongst others.

Maybe you've been lost, or you've run away, been kicked out, divorced, replaced, or banished from your pack. The loneliness that comes with being a lone wolf can be as isolating and cold as January. But learn from this time of being a lone wolf. Don't run and hide from it. Perhaps this season, brutal as it might be, is what you need to learn how to be alone — not because you were designed or deemed to be alone, but because you were meant to be OK and at peace with simply being you. And may everything that broke you be what helps you build your new pack. May all the pain you suffered be what fuels you to love your new fellow wolves deeper and more wholeheartedly. May the identity you lost in your former pack be redeemed through the affirmation you find in yourself and cherish in your new pack. There is a pack out there waiting for your wild, waiting to hear your howl.

I MARRIED A WOLF

I married a wolf. Ulrich. He is a German wolf who has lived up to his name, which means 'wolf power'. He is fierce, protective of his pack, and would do anything for the ones he loves. He is the kindest and most wise, creative, and thoughtful man I've ever known. He is everybody's darling, but he is a wolf: wild, untamable, loves to play, intensely fixated on his goals, watches over his territory, and when he howls the night skies become silent. Like a real wolf, he often communicates with his eyebrows. They used to scare me so much that I had to pretend they were furry caterpillars on his face. It is now a joke in his family, because they all have caterpillar-like eyebrows. But the main reason I call him my 'wolf' is because of the lessons I learned from him while learning to 'fight'.

When we first married, we were cooped up in a small, thirty-square-meter apartment in East Germany. We fought off mold like it was our job. We kept the blinds closed at all times from peeping neighbors, who at any point in the day would come up to our windows with their faces pressed against the glass to get a glimpse of what we 'outsiders' were up to. Daily, we braved showering in the prison-like basement where a deep, rusty, grey tub with no hot water sat at the end of a long hall, filled in the summer with more mosquitoes than a swamp — and I'm from Florida, I know.

To most, this might sound like a nightmare for anyone to live in, let alone newlyweds beginning their new lives together. But to us, it was home.

As we settled into our home more and more, so did we settle into our roles of being husband and wife. When you first get married, there is this strange cycle of patterns that tend

to develop. You're so excited to start your life together with someone and fill the role of being their spouse, and yet, you don't know yet what that role looks like. So, you start playing the part by pretending until either you figure it out, and authentically find your role, or something breaks.

In our first months of marriage, we fought so much. Maybe it was the normal adjusting to being newlyweds, and maybe it was the inevitability of two strong personalities coming from two very different cultures and backgrounds striving to co-exist together. Or maybe it was the mosquitoes, who knows, but we fought like hell. Well actually, I wouldn't say what we did was fighting, per se, more like attempting to fight, because neither of us really knew how fighting inside a marriage worked.

I am the classic child of divorce, who grew up in a home where disputes led to fights, fights led to separations, and separations led to divorce. My wolf is a child of parents still married. In his family, when they fought they would blow up at each other, run away, sleep on it, then come back the next day for breakfast, acting as if nothing happened, leaving nothing resolved or dealt with. Needless to say, neither of us were ever modeled a healthy way of fighting. Gradually, the pattern of fighting inside our marriage began to look like this.

Something would happen, normally insignificant. One of us would say or do something, and the other would react. Oftentimes they were normal reactions, tethered to the cultural response we both were raised to abide by, but to the other person they felt offensive and hurtful. For instance, you have no idea how rude "Would you mind taking out the trash?" sounds to a German and yet so polite to an American. And how frightening a thick German accent yelling about the trash sounds to an American.

When my wolf reacted to something hurtful I did to him, he explained his frustration to me in typical, direct German fashion, which at the time seemed like a snarling wolf with a fierce tongue and caterpillar-like eyebrows. This misunderstanding prompted me to respond with my own fangs, spitting out manipulative retorts to prove he was wrong. Cue my upbringing here, where it was ingrained in me that if we fought, it meant he would leave, and the only way to keep him was to prove he was wrong, which could convince him to stay. When I reacted to something hurtful my wolf did, I responded by shutting down, crying in my room and feeling deeply hurt. Meanwhile, his upbringing had trained him to ignore my reaction until it blew over. The next day when we would wake up, he'd kiss my forehead, and act like everything was fine, all while bottling up his emotions. Meanwhile, I was dealing with the inner turmoil of believing this man must not love me or want to stay in this marriage. Because if you fight, then you must not love each other. Right?

This pattern continued well into the first half-year of our marriage until one day, after we fought about something arbitrary, I slid down the fridge onto the cold kitchen floor, bawling my eyes out, and in my most broken state, I yelled, "Well I guess you're out, right? When are you going to leave me already?"

This response shocked and shook my wolf like nothing I'd ever seen. He stood over me, mortified and confused. But then in the sweetest, most loving voice he said, "Where am I going?" It had registered to my wolf that what our fights had been communicating to me was that he was unhappy in our marriage and wanted to leave, when in reality that couldn't have been farther from the truth. In the heat of the moment, he grabbed me, looked me straight in the eyes, and said, "I love you; I'm never going to leave you. Right now I am angry, and I am hurt because of the situation. I need time to process this, but I will come back to you and we will find a solution together."

As he walked away to process and cool down, I sat there alone on the floor feeling something unexpected: loved.

In the most intense, brawling of moments, he was able to pierce through my fears and pain and affirm his devotion to me, setting aside his own feelings to affirm mine. And in this moment of acceptance and security, something deeply broken inside me began to mend. It did not heal right then and there, but over time, through this new pattern of fighting on a foundation of committed love to one another, we began healing those broken patterns of the past.

Over the course of another year or so, our fighting pattern shifted. Every time we fought, my wolf, still with fangs and caterpillar eyebrows, would always end each fight by looking me in the eyes and saying, "I love you. I'm never going to leave you." He said it over and over and over until I believed it and no longer needed him to say it. And I no longer needed to manipulate, force, prove, or avoid the fight altogether, because my fears no longer narrated the conversation. I allowed my wolf the time he needed to calm down so that he could come back to me, and together, we could calmly figure things out. That made him feel respected and safe, freeing him from the need to bottle up and suppress his feelings. And over the years, fighting became something that scared us less and empowered our relationship more.

It's now been thirteen years of marriage, and although I daily need to hear "I love you," as does he, it's rare that I need to hear "I'm never going to leave you." Because now I believe, deep in my bones, that promise is real. I know there are no certainties in life, but I have found that my marriage, and my relationships in general, function and succeed far better when I believe the

promises made to me, rather than living in constant fear and distrust of them being lies. There is no room in love for fear and suspicion. There is no room to grow and take chances and build a life together when you are always waiting for your partner to leave, hurt or fail you.

It's easy to twist every mistake, every failure, every word your partner says into a validation of your fears. Consequently, it leaves little to no room for grace and acceptance of the weaknesses you both have. That kind of pressure and manipulation can bring any relationship to an end, married or not. Not necessarily because you two together couldn't work, but because your fears became a third party to your relationship, never giving it a fighting chance. And fighting, and knowing how to fight, is the only real chance such a close relationship has to survive.

Now when my wolf and I fight, we believe it will sharpen each other as individuals while also making us stronger as a couple and as a pack. Because we no longer see each other as enemies, we, like real wolves, benefit from the fighting done inside the safety of our pack, because it prepares us for external battles against our real enemies in life, who we now fight off together.

When we fight, it's not about breaking each other down, diminishing the individual in front of us until they conform to the person we want them to be. It's not about convincing them to react or agree with us, or even fight the way we want them to fight. It's about accepting each other and learning from one another, choosing to see the world from their perspective while still communicating our own. We confront each other to reform; we tackle issues to uncover unhealthy behaviors. And we speak up about our pain because we believe our pain matters to the other.

Often we remind each other that "it's more important to be loving than it is to be right." And by this, we do not mean that fighting is not loving or that we should keep our opinions and our perspectives to ourselves, just 'keeping the peace' and lying down submissively. That would be dehumanizing, chastising the voice and value of yourself or the one you love. That would be anything other than a lion. Instead, we mean that when we fight, we fight fair. We fight with humility, recognizing that our words have a power that can either build or destroy the person in front of us. Our truths might not be truths for the other. Our perspectives might not be law. And our bodies' gestures (especially our eyebrows), can create fear, which only leads to more brokenness.

It's very easy to be right in a fight. To stand your ground and protect your opinion with an iron fist and win. But at what cost are you willing to win? What value does protecting your loved one have in comparison to winning? It is so easy to win a fight, but it is not easy to be loving in a fight. To choose words that are righteous and constructive and not abusive and vindictive. To bring in perspectives that are helpful and not manipulative. To sometimes stick to your viewpoint, not because you are too prideful to back down, but because you genuinely believe this is what is best for both sides. To be more loving than to be right.

Though fighting with my wolf is still one of my least favorite things in the world to do, I no longer run from it, but welcome it. When we fight, it's not a warning sign for either of us that something is broken; it's an invitation for us to improve areas that need attention. And through the wrestling, confronting, and at times brawling through those issues, we improve. We become sharper individually and stronger together.

No one enjoys being confronted in areas they have faltered or failed in. It's humbling, threatens our pride, and when presented with thick German accents, is downright intimidating.

But when you realize the person confronting you is a wolf from your pack, who loves you and who is holding you accountable to be the lion you both believe you can be, then that confrontation becomes less threatening and more affirming. And affirmation mixed in with love becomes validation — validation of their commitment to you. As long as someone is committed to you, you realize that in the end, through fighting with someone you love, you become more loved.

THINGS I'VE LEARNED FROM WOLVES

- You must first know who you are on your own before you can belong to anyone or a pack.
- You should surround yourself with people who can fight with you to strengthen and sharpen your claws, not beat you down.
- When you fight inside a healthy, loving, respectful relationship, your fights can make your relationship stronger and bring you closer together.
- Knowing when to fight with someone and when to comfort someone is one of the wisest tools you can acquire.

"May the fighting you learn to do inside your pack of wolves prepare you for the battles you will conquer as a lion."

CHIPPED SHELLS

A tortoise's shell never becomes detached. It is attached from birth, and as a tortoise grows, so does its shell. The shell is made up of sixty different interconnected bones. Small, circle-like shapes called scutes (isn't that a cute word?) form over the outer shell, protecting the plates from injury and infection. Uneven growth of the scutes can cause the shell to become deformed, cracked, split, chipped or broken, just as bones can be. Tortoises also tend to have heavier shells than their turtle cousins, which weigh them down significantly and cause them to move extremely slowly. To compensate for their restricted movements, Tortoises are able to retract their heads, limbs and tails into their shells for protection when feeling threatened or attacked.

Before the age of two, I had two near-death experiences.

When I was six months old, my mother was coming home from work and stopped at the red light near our home. Suddenly a car came rushing past her, running the light and speeding away, and to her shock, she recognized the car as my father's. Immediately, she called to see what was wrong, and he said, "Get home quick; there's been an accident, and an ambulance is at our house. Lizzy is unconscious." My parents sped home to find the paramedics resuscitating me after I had been seizing and falling into a coma. They told my parents there was no time to wait. In the ambulance, we all went to the hospital. On the way, as my mother was holding onto me for dear life and praying for me not to go, the paramedics were able to bring me back. At the hospital, the doctors informed my mother that I had a severe allergic reaction, and if the emergency help had arrived any later, I would be dead.

About one year later, I was in a car accident. My sister, who was three and a half years old, and I, eighteen months old, were at our neighbor's house with a few other kids. At the end of the day, we were packed in her minivan to go home. She then ran inside with my sister for something while the rest of us waited in the car for their return. I patiently sat in an unstrapped seat in the back of a minivan parked at the tip-top of a narrow, steep driveway. One of the 4-year-olds in the car yelled, "Let's play taxi!" as he jumped into the front seat, put the minivan in neutral, and began steering the car. Just then, my sister and neighbor came out of the house, but they were too late.

The minivan started to roll backward; it picked up speed as it rolled down the steep driveway and eventually slammed into the curb, propelling me out of the window, headfirst into the ground, and rolling me into a ditch. All the other children in the car had minor injuries, However, my skull cracked, my teeth shattered, and I lay unconscious. Not long after, I was on my way to yet another hospital, this time with bleeding, swelling brain, and a concussion.

Both my experiences have had severe ramifications in my life. My health issues have caused many parts of my body and immune system to malfunction, leaving me with a lifetime of illness, reactions, and stress on my body. Not only did the later car accident give me a cracked skull, damage and shifting of certain organs, and years of repair on my teeth, but it also permanently affected my brain. My ability to process information, retain memories, and learn things properly were all hindered by my accident, leaving me with years of adjusting and working through both physical and learning disabilities such as my dyslexia.

School was challenging, eating was complicated, and daily activities were strenuous on my body and mind. I was constantly in and out of therapy sessions and tutors' and doctors' offices. Failing tests, falling behind in school, being teased, and missing out on activities were all constant reminders that I was burdened with the consequences of things that had happened to me.

Both as a child and well into my adult years, these health and learning issues not only burdened me physically but also emotionally. The insecurity of always feeling like I was broken and not working properly affected the way I valued myself. I never felt like I was enough and I thought I needed to work harder than everyone else only to be average. Over the years of not wanting to feel different, I found ways to hide and cover up my sickness and learning disabilities to the point that when actually I braved sharing about them, people didn't believe me and accused me of fabricating the story. This made the journey all the lonelier.

Like tortoises, I walked around with a body that has often felt like a shell. A shell I was not empowered by but burdened with. A burden that was too heavy and hard to carry — holding me back, slowing me down and making me feel different from everyone around me. Growing up, I often wondered why I couldn't trade my body in for a new, better-functioning model. Why was I the one doomed to live with a cracked shell? Why me?

When you walk around with that attitude toward your body, you will never become one with it. You never allow yourself to grow or be with it. You resist it. And when you resist your body, you resist yourself. And when you resist yourself, you resist your ability to live your life fully.

It took me years to accept my body's limitations. I would eat what I wanted and suffer the consequences on my fragile system. I would pretend I didn't have learning disabilities and not accept the help offered to me, secretly struggling through school and leading to nothing but more stress, anxiety and shame. I didn't want to accept that I had a shell.

It wasn't until I became a mother that I fully understood the gift of a chipped shell. Although adoption was always our plan for how we wanted to grow our family, one of the consequences of my health was being unable to bear children. My wolf and I adopted our daughter Bo Bei from China. At the time, the majority of children in need of homes had special needs. When we saw our daughter's file and read that she was visually impaired and would require extra support for medical needs, those things didn't turn us away; they drew our hearts closer to her. Bo Bei was three and a half when we adopted her and brought her home. She is by far the best thing that has ever happened to either of us, and I have learned so much from our time together. But it wasn't until a few months later that she helped me understand the beauty of carrying around my chipped shell and the pain it had caused me.

One night during story time, Bo Bei asked me about her eyes. After months of doctor appointments, new prescription glasses, therapy, and extra support around the house, her questions began to pile up. We laid there with her stuffed lion gripped tightly to her chest, the one we brought her on the day we met, and she said, "Mama, why are my eyes different?" The moment she asked me, I was reminded of my years of weeping with frustration over my own body and asking a similar question.

I paused for a moment, looked into her beautiful eyes, and said, "Because, like a tortoise, we have a shell that we live in -- our bodies. Everyone has a shell, and everyone's shell has problems at one point in their lives; let's call them 'chips.' Some chips heal, some don't. Some chips cause minor challenges, and some cause big ones. But everyone has chips, and we can either choose to see the chips as weaknesses or strengths. Your eyes are chipped, and that will bring you more challenges in life, but it will also bring you treasures. And you get to choose if you focus on the challenges or treasures." At that moment, she gripped tightly to her lion and my hand and whispered a prayer that challenged my pain and perspective on my own body, "I am thankful for my chipped eyes."

Everyone has a shell. Everyone has something in their life they've been burdened with carrying that they didn't choose. Whether it be a physical or mental disability or illness, a traumatizing experience, or some unfavorable inheritance you were born with, we all have shells, and we've all had damage done to our shells. Some shells may look only a little chipped while others display jagged cracks, but everyone has a shell.

A tortoise cannot shed its shell or trade it in for another if it becomes damaged or uncomfortable. No matter how heavy a burden it is, they must carry it around. They learn to move with it and develop with it, knowing that if they do not adapt and grow alongside the shell, they will be in tension with it, inevitably causing pain or even death.

Watching my daughter own her disability with honor and grace taught me to accept my body and the incredible abilities that came from my chipped, hefty shell. My learning disabilities prompted other parts of my brain to overcompensate. Over time, my right-brained, creative side began to function at a higher capacity. My health issues pushed me to engage more in food and health education. My emotional insecurities fostered my empathy for the hurt and broken people around me. My infertility opened up the world of adoption and lead me to my daughter. My near-death experiences gave me a deeper appreciation for life and seatbelts and championed me to write a book, something I never thought as a dyslexic would be possible. Knowing how to carry my chipped shell allows me to teach my daughter how to carry her own: forming me into the mother that my daughter needs.

We can choose to believe that we are prisoners to our shells, or we can use our shells to be empowered. We can take the hard, uncomfortable, ugly parts of our past, lives, bodies, and selves and believe they are weaknesses that will impair us. Or, we can grow into them and with them, allowing them to become the parts of us that make us strong and inevitably protect us. Just as the tortoise's shell is the most distinct and unique part of the animal, may you begin to see your flaws, hurts, and past in the same light. All these struggles that I have learned to accept have become valuable attributes that make me more human. They have become the qualities I love most about myself and treasures I have uncovered through carrying my chipped shell.

COMFORT SHELL

A tortoise's shell helps protect it from predators. When a tortoise feels threatened or at risk, it retracts its arms, legs and head quickly inside its shell, where it will stay secure until it feels safe enough to come back out. This incredibly durable armor is one reason that tortoises can outlive any other land animal on Earth, surviving in some instances up to a hundred and fifty years, if not longer! Thanks to this protection, tortoises can survive in many kinds of habitats and environments as long as they offer food and sustainable weather. If not, the tortoise will venture out to find a more promising ecosystem.

Growing up with my cracked shell of a body, I struggled to find my place. School was difficult and sports were exhausting, but the one area I always felt comfortable in was the arts. At four years old, while my family cheered at the football games for their favorite team, I sat on the sidelines drawing the crowd. By six I was obsessed with sewing together doll clothes and building ceiling-high doll houses out of boxes and makeshift items I found around our home. Then, on my eighth birthday, my father put a Baby Taylor guitar in my hands and my whole world changed.

Music became my outlet for my imagination and my emotions, as well as a way to process and make sense of my world. I learned to take all those insecurities and pain and confusion I felt as a kid growing up and put them into songs. I would come home from school crying about some bully or a boy who broke my heart, and after listening for some time, my mother would say, "Go to your room and write about it." I spent hours in my room writing songs, but everything changed the night I first performed one.

I was fourteen and my school was putting on a talent show. My friend signed us up to perform together what I thought would be a cover song. Only later did she inform me that she would be accompanying me on one of my own songs that I had written. There are not words to describe the amount of anxiety and fear that came with the idea of sharing one of my songs with anyone else. If having to sing or play guitar in front of people didn't scare me enough, letting anyone in on my secrets, stories, and private thoughts felt unbearable. I wanted to back out, but my friend said, "You've got something to say, and someone out there needs to hear it." So, I braved the invitation.

The night of the performance, I walked out on stage in front of an audience of a few hundred people and I panicked. I was so terrified that as I crouched down on the stool next to my friend, I slowly pulled my beanie over my eyes. My leg was shaking so much that my friend gently put her hand on it to slow it down; I think she feared it would put us off rhythm. There I was, hiding and shaking inside my beanie, much like a tortoise hides inside its shell from its predator. As the bright lights and many eyes focused on me, I closed my eyes, took a deep breath and played my song. At the end, it was dead silent. I just about ran off stage in fear that I had just made a huge fool of myself. But suddenly, a loud roar arose, and as I peeked my little eye out from my beanie, there in front of me was an audience filled with people standing and cheering for my performance. The beanie came off, the legs stopped shaking and my eyes were wide open.

From then on, I knew that I wanted to be an artist. I knew I wanted to play music, write and draw, and make people roar. And I knew that I wanted to figure out a way to use my art to make a difference in this world, but I had no idea where to start.

Fast forward a few years to the season before my 'escape' to Germany. A season that was incredibly uncomfortable, because everything about my life was seemingly comfortable. Right before the two-week period where my job, schooling, housing, relationships and many other things fell apart, every area of my life seemed to be working. So I thought. I had two steady paying jobs, a 4.0 grade point average in college (that's right, this dyslexic figured out how to do school), a performing band, a car, a roof over my head, a boyfriend and a community. On the outside, my life was full, but inside I'd never felt emptier. Here I was, plowing forward in so many areas of my life, and yet I had absolutely no idea what destination I was going to.

Living your life without an understanding of your purpose is not living, it's surviving. And when you are surviving, you're living to stay alive, not thriving with something to live for. Nothing in my life felt purposeful. I had no interest in what I was studying, but was merely sliding through school, making good grades because that was what was expected of me, not because I was passionate or had a plan for where this education was taking me. Work was paying my bills but not propelling me forward to any kind of significant carrier. My relationships lacked depth and empowerment, and my music and art felt void of reason. I was performing, playing shows, exhibiting my art, and yet it felt pointless and meaningless. That longing for purpose and understanding of what it was that I was supposed to be doing with my art gripped me and plagued my mind daily.

One night during this uncomfortable, 'comfortable' season of living in my hollow shell, I came home to find my roommate on the front porch of our house looking at her laptop, crying. When I asked her what was wrong, she said she was fine but turned the laptop around to me so I could see what she was looking at. There on the screen was a photograph that, little did I know, would change my life forever.

It was a portrait of a young Pakistani girl, dressed like a queen, wrapped in her traditional, tribal clothing with hands that knew the earth and eyes that had a story to tell. "What is this?" I asked my roommate as tears unexpectedly rolled down my own cheeks.

"It's a photography school in Germany that teaches you to take photos while traveling to different parts of the world. This is one of the photographs from the school." she said.

I didn't know how to respond, so I didn't. As I walked inside and went to my room, my roommate yelled from the porch, "The next photo school starts September eighth. Just so you know." I slammed the door in frustration and annoyance. But not at her. More at the confusion of how this photo could impact me so deeply.

As I lay down on my bed, I wrestled with this question. And I came to the conclusion that if something was speaking so strongly to me, then I must respond. Stomach turning, heart pumping, I said a prayer in the smallest of whispers, "I want to go to this school."

The next morning I woke up in a panic, and before I even got out of bed, I found myself yelling out, "There is no way I'm going! No way!" In this moment of fear and foolishness a small voice inside me, my lion if you will, asked me, "Why not?" I paused and reflected on that question for quite some time before listing all the reasons why uprooting my life, hopping on a plane and moving to Germany in a few weeks was not the most logical decision. There was school, work, community, my home, my jobs, not to mention I didn't even have a passport. The list was long: the list of all those very important, very responsible, very reasonable reasons to say no to going. In fact, they were really my hollow excuses to stay. Still, my answer was no. A tortoise cannot move unless it peeks its head and limbs out of its shell. Unless someone else does it for them.

I'm a firm believer that the callings on our lives are more committed to us than we are to them. And no matter what, they will do everything possible to get us to where we need to be, even if the journey there seems long and hard and even painful at times. Over the next two weeks, one by one all the things on my list of reasons to not go started to be erased. Well, more like killed off.

That Monday morning at ten a.m., registration for new fall courses for college opened up online. At 9.50 a.m. I was on the computer ready to sign up. At ten a.m., every single one of my courses was already fully booked. When I called my college to assess the situation, they said, "We are very sorry; all the courses you need to proceed are fully booked. You'll have to wait until next semester to take these classes."

The next day, my roommates held a meeting to inform me that they were canceling the lease on the house and moving out of town. That afternoon, my bosses from my two separate jobs called me to tell me they were letting me go, because they 'no longer had a need for me'. On Saturday, my band broke up and on Sunday my boyfriend dumped me.

Sunday night, I found myself in a parking lot after aimlessly driving around town in utter shock and disbelief. In a matter of seven days, every single area of my life had ceased to exist. As I got out of my car in a burst of rage, tears in my eyes, I yelled a prayer "What do you want from me?" And just then I noticed a sign on the car window next to me. All the letters had been wiped away but the date was remaining. September eighth. On the following Monday, I booked a flight to Germany.

Side note: September eighth not only was the start of the school, but I would soon come to find out it was my wolf's birthday.

I remember that when we touched down in Germany, I didn't want to get off the plane. I sat in my seat until I was the last person on board. That plane was like another shell for me, and I knew that whatever was outside my shell was going to change my life forever, and I wasn't ready for that. Eventually, after some convincing from the flight attendant, I did get off the plane. And as terrifying and hard as it was, taking that first step was one of the best decisions of my life.

Eventually I made it to my photography school. I'll never forget the conversation I had the first day with my instructors. "Hi, I'm Liz, and I'm not a photographer," I said.

Baffled and confused, they replied, "Then why are you at a photography school?"

To this I replied, "Because the photo you put online, advertising this school, moved me so much that it got me on a plane and moved me halfway across the world. I want to figure out how to do that with my music. I want to figure out how to use my music to move people. So I figured this school was the place to start."

With a smile and a chuckle they said, "I think you're in the right place."

The photo school was six months long. Three months were devoted to learning how to use photography to serve others and three were devoted to applying that knowledge out on the field in different countries. I ended up on a team that went to Chad to volunteer in a village that sheltered women and children who were victims of the war in Darfur.

When we arrived, I was overwhelmed by the despair around me. There were women who had been beaten, assaulted, raped and forcefully circumcised against their will. Their children had been captured by the rebel soldiers and if rescued and brought back, they were missing limbs and eyes and were psychologically traumatized. The level of massacre and misery paralyzed me. I had no idea how to help. I was not a counselor, a doctor, not even a humanitarian. I was an artist. What good did I have to offer?

After a few weeks of serving in the village with practical

work and other various activities that felt arbitrary and pointless to me, though I'm sure well intended by our team, a pastor from the village asked my team and me if we wanted to join them for a service. We agreed and shuffled into a small church packed with women from the village. The pastor got up and shared his message and then out of nowhere he turned to our team and said, "Would anyone here like to play a song for the ladies?" My team leader, without hesitation, literally pushed me to the front of the room. The pastor placed a four-stringed guitar in my hands and there I was, yet again, standing in front of a crowd of people waiting on me to perform. But this time, I didn't have my beanie. I didn't have my shell.

I closed my eyes and sang on repeat the first word I could think of: "Hallelujah". Moments later, I heard it again, that roar. But this time, it wasn't an applause, it was wailing. I opened my eyes to a room full of women crying and screaming as they began to roll on the floor, crouching down on their knees, waving their hands in the skies. I was honestly frightened and had no idea what was happening. I looked to the pastor for clarity and he looked back at me, tears in his eyes and said, "Just keep playing." So I did. I kept playing and playing until eventually they told me I could stop.

When I got off stage, the pastor came up to me and said, "Do you have any idea what you've done?"

I apologized. "I'm so sorry, I don't."

He explained. "In this culture, these women do not cry. They don't allow themselves to. We've been trying for so long to get them to open up about their pain and hurt, so we can help them process and heal, but they just wouldn't. They won't allow themselves to express their pain. Your music just allowed them to do this. It's the first time we've ever seen them cry. Thank you."

The magnitude of this moment changed everything for me. I knew that even though I didn't know how, or when, or where, I wanted to use my music to serve the broken. For so many years my music was about my own, personal, broken shell. My stories and my life. But there were so many other stories, and lives, and broken shells out there that needed to be heard, and needed to be given a platform. And if I could offer that, then I wanted to do everything in my power to make that happen.

After a few more weeks of serving in the village, and eventually evacuating because the war spread into our territory, we returned to Germany. I came back with a fire in my belly — not only from the parasites I obtained on my travels, but from passion. A passion I had been waiting for my entire life. A passion for how to use my art to make a difference in this world. And much to my surprise, when I returned, I found many others from the school, including my soon-to-be wolf, who shared my passion.

One thing led to another, and we took the concept we learned from our photo school and started a non-profit organization that would use art to serve people in extreme poverty. Vision turned to action and action turned to impact. Over the next fifteen years, we traveled around the world using all different forms of art to serve people in all different nations. From photography to music, Ethiopia to India, film-making to painting, China to Afghanistan. We partnered with locals to start and support projects that helped serve people in extreme poverty.

We microfinanced small businesses to empower various widows, victims of human trafficking and the homeless to be self-sufficient. We helped form rescue centers for children who were going to be killed due to tribal and cultural beliefs. We created sponsorship programs for orphans and at-risk kids, and provided them with education and basic needs. We arranged many operations and medical needs for those in need, helped influence laws to be passed that protected the innocent and supported locals to rise up and take action in their own villages and neighborhoods. And we did it all through the arts.

We packed our bags and guitar cases and went to the ends of the Earth to find stories and give them a platform to be heard. We believed that everyone had a voice, and everyone had a story, and if we could use our art and music to highlight those stories, then others would have the opportunity to listen, respond, and create change. Wherever we went, we did art. Whether it was hanging photos in galleries in Paris or in the slums of India, we shared stories. Whether we were playing concerts for thousands on the streets of China, or rock shows in the landfills of Addis Ababa powered by generators, we shared stories. We partnered with locals in their countries and we partnered with locals from our countries. And through the art, change was made. During this time I created 'Liz and the Lions'. My band-turned-mantra was the driving force behind my vision. My 'lions' started out as my fellow band members, and 'my wolf' that toured the world with me, playing shows and using CD sales and concert tickets to finance and raise awareness for these projects. I called them lions because I wanted to surround myself by people who were wild, dangerous, and fierce like real lions. And that's exactly who they were. But over the years I felt there was more to the story of the lions than was confined to just our band.

Like the night of the talent show, shaking in fear under my beanie until I heard the roar, and again in the village in Chad in that room full of women roaring, I wanted to hear roars. Not for me, not for my music. Through my music I wanted to empower people to become like lions and I wanted to help them roar.

Over the years Liz and the Lions expanded into the brand Live as Lions and became the theme to my calling: empowering others. Whether it was sixteen-year-olds in Ethiopia or sixty-year-olds in America, I wanted to help people roar. I wanted to help them take their cracked, broken shells and make something beautiful out of them. I wanted them to share their stories and use their talents and gifts to make a change in this world. I wanted them to believe in their voice and to use it to roar louder than the pain and the brokenness.

It's been over a decade and a half since I took that first step off the plane, the one that changed the course of my life — that first step that at the time felt impossible to take. But here is the thing about steps: when you take them one at a time, they build on one another. And eventually, the more you take, the higher you go and the more comfortable you are with taking them. And it doesn't matter how long you might need to take each step — after all, like a tortoise, slow and steady wins the race, right?

For so many years I was terrified to leave my comfort zone. I didn't believe I was brave enough, strong enough, smart enough, or talented enough to step outside the world in front of me. It was a world that my society, my community and my fears told me I was bound to. A world limited to the parameters that my talents, education, and zip code extended to. A world limited to my courage, or lack thereof.

I do not believe some people are born braver than others. I believe circumstances produce bravery, through situations that you either face unwarrantedly that you choose to be in. I do not believe you can live a purposeful life without risk or without chance. Without making yourself vulnerable to the fate of this world, you will always shelter yourself from it, never really living it. However, I do believe that every time life presented me with an opportunity to say yes to risk, and I took it, it rewarded me with growth: growth in my character, my relationships, my career, my art, my dreams, and certainly in my courage.

The life I have lived since that first step is nothing like I could have ever imagined. It has brought me to places on the map in over 40 nations I never dreamed my feet would touch. It has educated, inspired, and challenged me in ways I never thought possible, and humbled me in areas I never knew I needed. However, stepping out of my comfort zone has also led me to many failures in my life.

As I said, in the pursuit of finding out who I was and what I was called to do on this Earth, I took a lot of risks. Some succeeded, but many failed. Many projects and programs my team and I created did not work, and some even caused more damage than good. But we did not retreat back into our shells after these failures; we tried again — and again, and again, until we got them right. Many relationships I pursued outside my comfort zone ended sourly, painfully, or brokenly. I learned from them, and took what I learned and grew healthier relationships. Many dreams I chased, chased me into defeat. I chased them back until I caught bigger ones and became better, stronger, and wiser from them.

The more I learned to be comfortable outside the shell of my comfort zone, the more comfortable I became in general with risk. When I look back at being the little girl who squealed over cockroaches growing up in Florida, I chuckle in comparison to the monsters and beasts I have faced along my journeys. I think of sleeping in landfills with homeless children and the odor from their sounder of swine, being sniffed in my sleeping bag by a wild leopard, chased by a family of wild boar, escaping hyenas, or the countless nights waking up beside far too many snakes, rats, and spiders. From being hijacked by tribal men to being airlifted out during war, from being held in jail cells in two foreign countries to flying through not one, but two hurricanes.

Every single one of those situations was unintended, unwelcome, and an unexpected risk that came as a consequence to saying yes to living outside my comfort zone and pursuing the calling on my life. If you had told me on that plane, many moons ago, that those risks were waiting ahead for me, I never would have gotten off the plane. Never. But looking back, none of these things stopped me from moving forward. They terrified me, derailed me at times, and even put me in a few counseling sessions. But none of them stopped me. In surviving each one of them, they inevitably made me brave.

Tortoises are survivalists. They know when to stick their heads out and move forward, and when to retreat. They know when to leave an environment that isn't serving them any more and they know when to stay. People who know when to retreat and when to move forward, even outside their comfort zone, are not built braver, they just live more bravely. You will never know what or who is outside your shell unless you stick your head out and take the first step. Your shell is there to protect you, support you, and empower you, not to hold you back or limit you.

THINGS I'VE LEARNED FROM TORTOISES

- When you've become too complacent and comfortable inside your world, you're no longer challenging yourself, and therefore you're no longer growing.

- Stepping outside your comfort zone by doing something that terrifies you can only make you braver. Even if you fail.

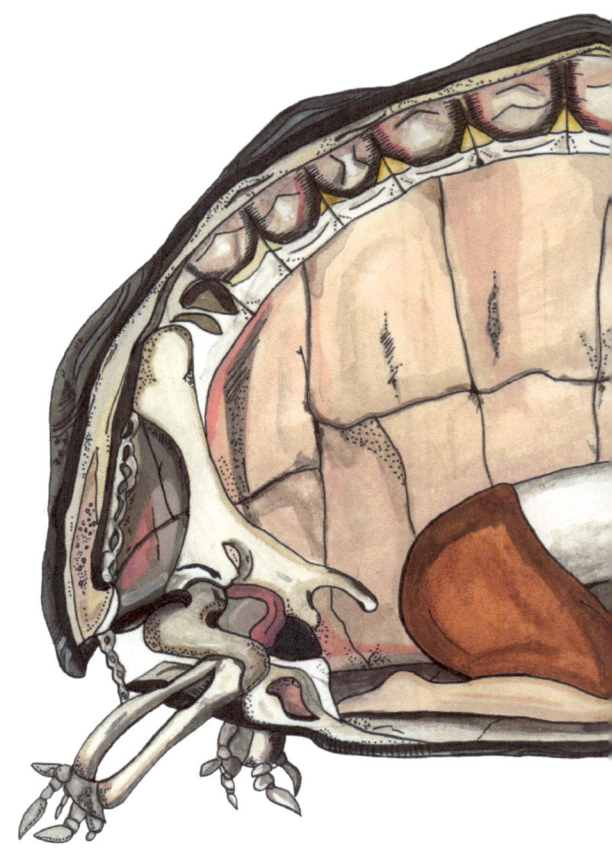

- You cannot change the shell you were born with, but you can choose how you use it. Hide inside its limitations or grow with it and use it to strengthen you.

    "May the chipped, broken shell of the tortoise shield and protect the lion in you as you step out of your comfort zone and into your calling."

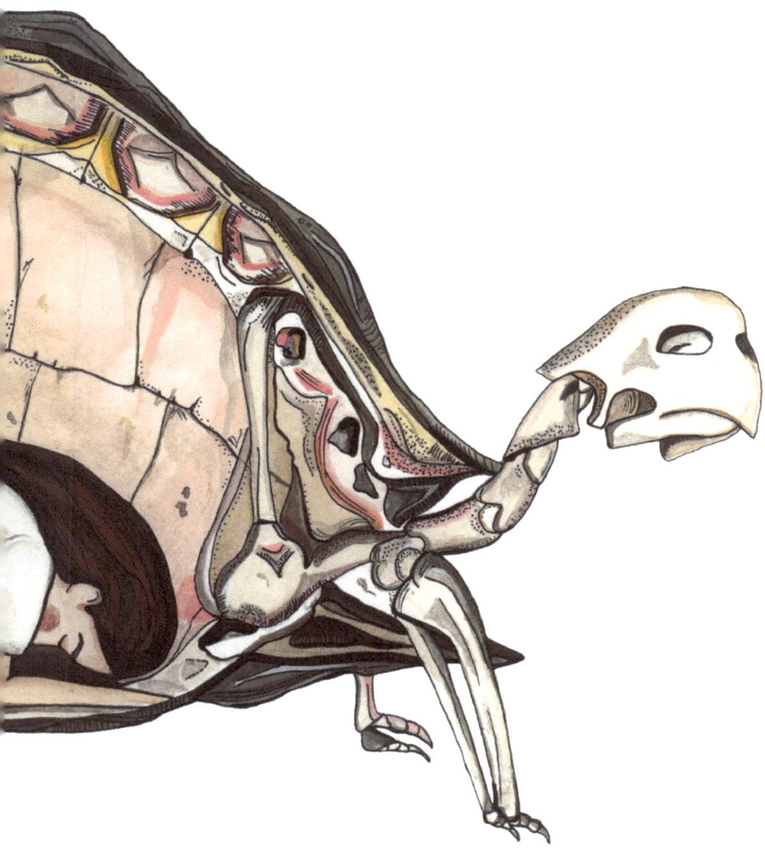

POSSUMS

POSSUMING OUT

Opossums are very adaptable and flexible animals, enabling them to survive in a variety of habitats. opossums give birth to up to two litters of four to eight babies, or joeys. After a thirteen-day gestation period, when joeys are born, they immediately crawl inside their mother's pouch where they remain for up to fifty days. They then exit the pouch and spend their juvenile days clinging to their mother's back. Once fully grown, possums leave their mothers to go live solitarily and nomadically. When opossums 'play possum,' they sometimes flop onto their sides and lie on the ground with their eyes closed, or stare fixedly into space. They extend their tongues and generally appear to be dead. They bare their teeth, begin to foam saliva around their mouths, and a foul-smelling fluid secrets from their anal glands (gross!). Their stiff bodies can be prodded, turned, or even picked up without them having any reaction. These animals can typically regain consciousness after a period of anywhere from a few minutes to a few hours.

"Pretending conflict doesn't exist does not keep the peace; it only leads to more destruction."

There is nothing quite like the pain of people abusing you, except when the people you trust most stand idly by while it happens. When the people you look to for support or even protection freeze up like a possum when faced with conflict, seeming to 'play dead' by actively not interfering with controversy, even at the expense of your wellbeing, it is devastating. Although trying to navigate that kind of pain and neglect can feel impossible and even unfair, I have personally found it helpful and even healing to try and make sense of this opossum-like behavior.

So let me tell you a story about my experience with 'opossums'.

Once upon a time, there were friends-turned-foes in my life who hurt me deeply. For the sake of the story, let's call them 'beasts'. And through this time of pain and suffering, I confided in a close friend to help get me through this hard time; let's call them my 'opossum'.

My opossum, who I loved deeply, was there for me in ways I couldn't have imagined, but ways that I always hoped a friend would be. They helped me feel safe and loved during a season in which I felt anything but. Because I trusted my opossum more than anyone else, day in and day out I shared with them the hurt and pain that the beasts brought me. I shared intimate and vulnerable parts of myself and my heart only with them. I was so grateful for their loyalty and friendship that I came to depend on it to get through that season. As time went on, my opossum revealed to me that they, too, were being hurt by the beasts and also began to fear them. This shared pain that we carried brought us closer together. Like baby opossums clinging to their mother's backs for survival, so did we cling to each other to get through this season. Through this support, I began to believe that our shared hurt would help us find a way out of this challenging season and rise above the abuse of the beasts, together. Until one day, I realized that my opossum — my loyal, faithful friend — had also been a loyal, faithful friend to the beasts all along.

This revelation hurt me profoundly, and I doubted my trust in my opossum. I began to question everything. Were the beasts controlling my possum and coercing their loyalty? Was my opossum lying to me the whole time in order to gain something for themselves, or even the beasts? Was my opossum being honest with me about their pain, but was too scared of the beasts to admit it to them? Or, did my opossum never feel hurt or suffering at the hands of the beasts, but allowed me to think they did in order for me to feel supported and not alone?

I wanted answers to these questions that plagued my mind, so I approached my opossum directly. Much to my dismay, when I began to ask that they explain themselves, my opossum froze. They became completely and utterly incapable of giving me direct answers to any of my questions. Nothing they said made any sense. There was so much fear and anxiety in my opossum that it almost felt as if these questions were staring at them like a predator ready to attack. When I asked, "What's going on? Why are you responding like this?" I'll never forget their reply.

"I'm possuming out."

Just as real opossums will 'play possum' by falling into a comatose-like state when triggered by stress, so did my friend admit they were 'possuming out' in a similar fashion. The pressure that came from our conflict caused the same reaction; they felt paralyzed to respond, fearing what might happen. It was as if my opossum was cast in some kind of frozen spell and nothing I said could break them free.

As the days went on and the abuse from the beasts became worse, my opossum continued to 'possum out', and I began to pull away. I hoped some distance would help my opossum understand the consequence of their actions and bring them closer to me. Maybe remembering the warmth of our friendship would melt them out of this frozen spell and raise them up like a lion to come to my rescue and defend me from the burly beasts. But it didn't. Eventually, I just left. Like baby opossums who crawl away from their mothers (often when she is in the middle of one of these paralytic states) to live alone and nomadically, so did I eventually crawl away from the comfort and support I once clung to in my opossum friend, and went to live away from all the pain and hurt the beasts and the opossum caused.

I would like to tell you that this story ended happily ever after. That my opossum eventually snapped out of their paralysis and came to defend my honor. That the ruthless beasts were taken down and righteousness and justice prevailed. But the truth is, none of that happened. Maybe one day it will, but perhaps not.

Through this journey of dealing with opossums and beasts, I have come to learn that in our relationships, trying to 'keep the peace' at the cost of honesty can backfire and cause even more damage. Like opossums, if we fear the presence of tension, we will be tempted to stay neutral, freeze, and withdraw from the conflict, person, and even environment. We 'possum out' when the love for peace temporarily or permanently overrides our ability to assert ourselves in a vital conflict. This fear of discomfort creates a barrier not only between us and a healthy solution, but also between us and the people involved. Inevitably, isolating ourselves from conflict can also isolate those we love, leaving them to deal with it alone. And in some cases it can eventually separate us from them permanently.

To this day, I don't know what happened with my opossum. I have no idea if our relationship was real and meant the same to them as it did to me. I don't know if I clung too tightly to them, causing them too much stress and anxiety. I have no idea if, in their version of this story, I was actually the beast and my beasts were actually their friends. Or if they loved us all equally but didn't know how to confront any of us about our actions, and felt caught in between. I've assumed, considered and processed every angle I can imagine, but I have no real answers since my opossum is gone.

What I do know is that in spite of all the pain the beasts caused me — and believe me, it was tremendous —- the pain that 'possuming out' caused was worse. I don't say that to attack my opossum. I still love them very much, have forgiven them and want nothing but the best for them. I say this to explain the immense consequences that can come from choosing to abandon or avoid relationships when conflict arises, and the pain it brings when you freeze and 'play possum.'

We all know opossums, and we've all been one at some point or another. We've all backed down from a fight, chosen not to speak up, neglected defending someone we loved, and avoided confrontation to keep our peace of mind. And to an extent, that is normal. You don't need to (and shouldn't) assert yourself in every conflict. But you also don't need to avoid every conflict either. When avoiding conflict becomes a reflex, it's a sure sign that conflict is something you fear. And as we know, unresolved fear does not dissolve; it builds.

From my experience, when we 'possum out' to keep the peace around us, it often comes with a void of peace on the inside. Always trying to keep the peace, please others, stay loyal, be liked, and do good can be more exhausting, and cause more internal conflict than the actual battle going on around you. The stress manifested in opossum behavior can potentially build up so much that there can be severe ramifications on one's psychological and physical health, or even boil up so intensely that it eventually explodes back out in unhealthy behaviors.

A short temper, lashing out, passive-aggressive comments, erratic behavior: they can all be the result of internalizing conflict, letting it fester and build until it bursts back out of you into the world in which you tried so hard to maintain peace. This cycle that 'opossums' go through must be exhausting, and ultimately counterproductive. In the end, this method of keeping the peace seems to lead to far more agony than anyone should go through simply because they fear confrontation.

Internalizing your fear, hurt, and pain does not eliminate them from your life, it only transfers them from one place to the other. Allowing that much fear of confrontation to rule your life will only isolate you from living it and from being with others. Like opossums who once lived in the comfort of a pack, and now live alone and isolated and in constant fear of predators, so will you live if you continue to build your life around the avoidance of confrontation. For this world is not void of conflict. Love, intimacy, and connection with others is not void of conflict, it is shaped by it. Remember what we learned from wolves — conflict, when resolved in a healthy and empowering way, can lead us to more true peace and harmony in our lives.

So let us stop 'possuming out.' Let us learn to 'lion up' by facing our fear of conflict dead on and actively engage in trying to resolve it. And though we might not always feel strong enough, smart enough or even brave enough to conquer conflict, it is better to live in a world where we are trying to overcome our fear of confrontation rather than letting that fear overcome us. Pretending conflict does not exist ultimately does not keep the peace; it only leads to more destruction, pain, and brokenness within our lives, our relationships, and our society.

PEACEMAKERS VS PEACE LOVERS

Opossums live in temporary, ready-made, abandoned burrows and put little to no effort into building their own homes. Being nocturnal, they favor dark, secluded burrows during the daytime. They are also scavengers who often raid trash cans and dumpsters for leftover food. When threatened, opossums will 'play possum' by mimicking the appearance and smell of a sick or dead animal in order to fool a predator into leaving it alone.

For those of us fighting for goodness and justice in a world filled with monsters and beasts, we value the prevailing of peace: peace that looks like freedom, security, and harmony that can be found within ourselves, our relationships, and society. We believe peace is not only essential for life, but a purpose we must all seek and strive toward. But what happens when we need to go into battle or conflict to have peace? What happens when we must face adversities, friends, and beasts in order to create peace?

Too often, we believe that peace is the absence of conflict and disputes, when often those things are actually crucial to the outcome of reconciliation and harmony. When it comes to preserving peace, I have come to find that there are two types of roles — that of a peacemaker and that of a peace-lover.

A peace-lover is a lover of peace. They value keeping the peace through the preservation of harmony and serenity, and believe that peace can be maintained through keeping conflict absent from their lives. This sense of stability is essential for peace-lovers to feel that they can survive amid the chaos around them. To keep this peace at all times, peace-lovers often stand idly by when faced with any adversity — refusing to engage or involve themselves in any conflict between them and anyone else, hoping to preserve the peace, whether it be a matter of dispute in which they are personally involved, or one of injustices occurring around them. To engage in conflict would, according to their belief system, bring about the destruction of peace. Therefore, the avoidance of conflict will result in the preservation of peace.

Peacemakers, on the other hand, are those who see the need to create peace by reconciling adversaries. They believe that peace can only be created through actively finding a solution, even if that involves participating in conflict through the process. When convicted by the need to create peace, peacemakers often refuse to back down when faced with oppression or injustice and march forward, regardless of the unconscionable pain, danger, opposition or defeat they might face on the journey toward peace. Whether it be in their own lives, family, relationships, society, or even government, peacemakers believe that in order to fight for goodness and justice one must insert themselves in areas where there is a lack of peace, bringing solutions of reconciliation and justice.

Am I a peace-lover or a peacemaker?

When I think of the daily confrontations in my life, in figuring out whether or not I am being more of a peacemaker or peace-lover, I ask myself, "Am I being more like a lion or an opossum?" I am more like a lion when I am striving to make peace, and willing to 'lion up' by actively asserting myself in situations of injustice by trying to pave the way to future peace. I am more like a opossum when I 'possum out' by avoiding conflict, to preserve peace and harmony in my own life.

I think most of us would like to believe that we are lions, peacemakers. That when faced with evil, injustice, or unfairness around us or directly to us, surely we would rise and fight for goodness. But how often in our lives do we find the courage and strength to rise? And to what extent and expense are we willing to do so? Which conflicts are we called to and willing to engage in? And how are we going to actually make peace?

It is difficult to know how to experience peace, let alone make it. Through the news, social media, and uproar of critics around the world, it feels like everywhere you turn someone is asking you to join their cause, be on their team, and rally for what they deem most important. From fighting global warming to ending animal cruelty, from poverty to human trafficking, from civil rights to war — if you engage, they feel supported and championed on their voyage to justice. If you deny them, if you dare defer the invitation to join, you are seen as an enemy, or worse, an apathetic perpetrator of injustice.

One reaction to this problem is to simply do our best to help everyone, just a little. We see the need to contribute to peace in the world, but we don't know where to start, so we begin to say yes to many opportunities that come our way. We crack the door open for anyone advocating their concerns. We skim every article, like every post, and grab every pamphlet coming our way. We are open to hearing about the magnitude of injustice and want to participate in making this world a better place. But not too much. Just a little. Just enough to feel involved, but not enough to feel the weight of responsibility for so many causes at once. Because hey, if everyone helps out a little, it helps out a whole lot, right?

Before long, we have a huge stack of pamphlets in the corner of the kitchen; we feel a twinge of guilt for that latte we bought, knowing there are people in the world who don't even have clean water; we regret liking that one post, because the next day it was debunked as misleading and ill-informed. And so, the perpetual attempts to 'help a little', please everyone a little, and give a little, become a vicious cycle of us trying not to feel numb while attempting to engage enough to keep our peace of mind. And all the while, not truly feeling like we are making any real change in this world.

Another reaction to the overwhelming requests for action is to fully commit ourselves to being a lion, a true peacemaker. What often happens, to those bold and passionate few who are willing to step up and take action, is that we begin to see injustice everywhere, and feel the need to fight everything. We dive in and try and help out everywhere there is a need. Everyone has that one friend — you know who I mean. The one who seems to 'fight the good fight' constantly, and every week it's for some new cause. They're freeing the whales on Saturday, picketing at the borders on Sunday, saving the rainforests on Monday and leading the charge for female equality by Friday.

Let me be very clear here. These people can be obnoxious. They can be overenthusiastic. And they can certainly be incredibly annoying. But these are also some of my favorite people in the world. As inconsistent and irritating as these people and their charges might seem, I think we need them. I, for one, would rather be in a world filled with these inconsistent peacemakers than those who are too numb to care.

That being said, however, exhausting oneself for every cause, every day, is ultimately ineffective in the long term. When we are not properly equipped, educated, and prepared to tackle the injustices in the world, our efforts can sometimes lead to more harm than good, and open us up for intense, and sometimes deserved, criticism.

Knowing how to be an effective, change-creating peacemaker takes many years of trial, error, and education. And yet, far too often, when lions dare to rise out of the comfort of being a lover of peace to take charge and try to make peace, they are attacked and slandered for their attempts. Frequently, it is from the opossums. The choice to become a lover of peace and 'possum out' can oftentimes lead you to being one of those that are loudest against peacemakers, even those who are capable of creating real and good progress against injustice.

These are the opossums who hide outside the fight, mocking and shaming those who are trying their best to do good. Because to a peace-lover, anyone who asserts themselves is simply creating more chaos, like a poison that must be stopped. So they taunt and devalue the efforts of the peacemakers, but often not directly, since a peace-lover by nature would never confront someone head on; that would require conflict. No, they engage through the privacy and support of their comfort zone, giving their opinions from a comfortable distance.

They are the teenage trolls of the internet, chatterbox grannies of the country club, archaic bureaucrats of our governments and the spoiled privileged, who believe that any effort made by others to make change in this world will offset the balance of consistent peace they strive to keep in their lives.

They hide behind passive-aggressive comments, sarcasm, social media retorts, dislike buttons, and unyielding viewpoints that position themselves as neutral and impartial — allowing the prevailing injustice to perpetuate around them by blocking any attempt at reform or change attempted by their peers.

And yet, these frustrating, anti-change types do not always fit into the opossum stereotype we imagine they belong in. Some of them were lions once. And they became so worn out, neglected, tormented, abused and unsupported by the opossums of this world that their efforts to create peace burnt them out, exhausted them, and broke them into opossums. It's the exhausted social workers who, after years of doing good, have not seen the fruits of their labor. The overworked teachers who are unappreciated, underpaid, and unserved. The isolated mothers, unsupported humanitarians, silenced scientists and teenage activists who have all set out to help others, and have been chewed up and spit back out. They are wounded, hurt, and bitter from years of giving and seeing little in return. These once world-changing lions are sometimes at the highest risk of 'possuming out'.

In reality, at some point in our lives, we will be peace-loving opossums, and we will be peacemaking lions. I, for one, have been both. I was the annoying teenager playing benefit concerts for hurricane survivors on Friday, serving the homeless on Sunday, and trying to get everyone in my neighborhood involved by Monday. In my mid-twenties, I was actively campaigning for projects around the world that served the poor and needy, while confusing 'likes' on social media with affirmation of my work. In my early thirties I burnt out. I had spread myself too thin, leaving myself exhausted and bitter toward anyone who thought they could change the world.

After years of working in nonprofits, developing countries and with at risk people, there came a time in my life when the weight of the world had become far too much for me. All I wanted was to flop over, 'play possum' and not engage. The injustices and oppression I had seen, and the little support I had, overwhelmed and devastated me until I felt powerless and hopeless. In that state, I could do nothing but retreat, and strive to find peace around me. If you had a cause, an issue, or a problem in your life, the response that boiled within me was, get away from me; I cannot handle it! I felt dead to the needs of the world. 'Possuming out' became my safety. It was my survival. But what I found, in this state of needing and desiring peace, is that peace became like an idol in my life. I valued it above all else and blocked off everything and everyone that threatened it. When you're a peace-loving opossum, there is nothing more important than keeping the peace, to the point that it blinds you to injustice and the needs of those around you.

The longer I stayed in this state of worshipping peace, the less I became. The less I engaged in the good and bad around me, and the number I became. The less aware and informed I was about the world I lived in, the more ignorant I became. I became uncompassionate toward others, less involved, less active, less alive, and ultimately apathetic to the injustices around me.

When the world overwhelms us with its pain and brokenness, we retreat into the safety and comfort of what we find peaceful in our lives. That is normal, and that is necessary. Did you know that male lions sleep for twenty hours a day to disengage and regain strength before rising for battle? Females need significantly less rest, but we don't need to go into our superiority right now. What we can learn, from strong, powerful, fearless lions, is that they know when to fight, and when to rest.

Retreating, resting, getting re-equipped and resetting our focus and priorities is necessary to be able to serve others. It's about knowing when to back down from your battle and take rest like a lion, instead of playing dead like an opossum. And the key to knowing when to back down is understanding your strengths, as well as when and how to use them.

I remember coming home from a long trip to India, where I had been volunteering at a children's home in the rural area of Vijayawada, and the overwhelming consequences of poverty and injustice hit me more than ever before. I called my sister and told her how hopeless I felt, because there was so much need, and so much work, and so many places to serve and give, and I didn't know where to begin. The pressure made me feel like a failure before I even started. I'll never forget the advice she gave me. She said, "This world is filled with problems. There will always be problems. But you have to figure out which problem you are most passionate about. And when you do, you spend the rest of your life learning how to solve that one problem. You put all your time, effort, resources, skills, talents, and education into the solution for that problem. And then, eventually, you will see change, real change. And if everyone did that, then we would see real, global change, wouldn't we?"

My sister is an environmental policy maker. She saw the problems in our environment and the effects they have on our planet, and has spent her life and career trying to solve those problems. Or as my nephews (her boys) like to say, "Mom's saving the polar bears!"

It was after this conversation that I began to grasp an essential concept — a truth we must understand if we want to avoid exhaustion and 'possuming out.' It is that we must have an accurate and distinct understanding of our individual role as a lion. Your purpose, or your 'calling' as I like to say, is really just figuring out who you are, what gifts you possess, and how you can take all of that and be of use to something in this world that you deem important. Something that gets your blood boiling, or your heart pounding, that makes you so passionate that you will do everything in your power to further its cause. Whether it be fighting human trafficking, raising little humans, or producing ethically-sourced paper clips — if it's a problem you feel passionate about, and solving will bring good to the world, I say we need it!

We need lions on this Earth more than we need opossums. We need you. We need your ideas and your voice. We need your opinions and solutions. We need you to engage and play an active part in making this world a better place. We need you to speak up when you see something wrong, be it in your relationships or the world around you. We need you to make conscious decisions in your life to stay balanced, healthy and effective, so you don't 'possum out' on us, for we need you to rise like a lion, standing up to the injustice and monsters and beasts of this world to create real peace on Earth.

When lions fear their territories, communities or lives are at stake, they roar to ward off other predators and if necessary, they engage with physical conflict to protect their own. Opossums on the other hand have no loyalty to anything other than themselves. From a young age they live nomadically, solitarily wandering through the world around them. They live in trees or with comfort and warmth in abandoned homes and burrows that were once dug up and belonged to animals who invested and labored for their existence. The peace and comfort that we experience every day in our homes, neighborhoods, laws, countries and planet, has always come from the sacrifice and

expense of those who braved first to fight for it. We can decide to claim our territory as treasured inheritance, or exploit and prosper from it. But if you continue to live in this world, without engaging in it, and fighting for its prosperity, you will live like a opossum lives inside someone else's home: comfortable, but not deserving. It won't fit you. It won't bring you peace. Because you can only enjoy the comforts of peace after the engagement of conflict to gain it has been accomplished. And you, my friend, were never created to live as a peace-loving opossum in this beautiful world we've been given. You were created to claim it, and fight for it, like a lion.

Compressed point: we need you to invest in the areas around you, like lions who claim their territory, protect their lands and build their community around them. We need you to not live like opossums who wait around for others to do the work and live comfortably and quietly in the abandon homes of the veterans.

THINGS I'VE LEARNED FROM POSSUMS

- Choosing not to engage in conflict or confrontation does not make the problem go away.
- When you witness injustice, harm or any kind of offense happening and you stay silent, you are not keeping the peace, you are affirming the injustice.
- When keeping peace in your world becomes more important to you than anything else, peace can oftentimes become an ideal that your life becomes enslaved to. Slavery to anything will eventually lead to a lack of freedom. And a life without freedom will inevitably be a life without peace. Learn to make peace, rather than keep it.
- When battling for peace, it is important to know when to rest like a lion so you don't play dead like an opossum. It is easy to criticize those trying to make peace in the world, and much harder to join them.

   "May you learn to not play dead like an opossum, but step up like a lion."

MOTH INFESTATION

Toneola bisselliela, also known as 'clothes moths', are pests that can destroy fabric and other materials. They feed on certain materials that contain a fibrous protein called keratin that the worm-like larvae of the clothes moth can digest (yummy!). Severe infestations of clothes moths can develop undetected in certain environments, like your home, causing irreparable harm to vulnerable materials. Adult female moths are capable of laying anywhere between a hundred to four hundred tiny eggs, typically 0.5 mm long. These eggs hatch into larvae, and this is the infamous destructive stage. Clothes moth larvae can eat away at materials at this stage for up to thirty months (two and a half years!) while waiting for the right conditions to turn into adult moths.

Like no one wants to throw away their favorite rug, no one wants to throw away a friendship or a job they've invested in.

Have you ever had a moth infestation in your home that resulted in you disposing of forty-two large trash bags filled with more than half of your belongings? Well, I have, and although at the time it felt like a nightmare, it turned out to be one of the best lessons I ever learned.

About a month before the infestation, I kept having this feeling that something was 'off' with our home. At the time we were living in a five-story walk up, pre-war apartment (now in the southern half of Germany), which by all aesthetic standards was a lovely place to live. But something felt off, as if there was something there that shouldn't be, and I couldn't quite figure out what it was. From what I could see, everything looked fine. Nothing was wrong — no need to look deeper. Time went on and life was busy as usual, so I pushed this feeling aside.

A few days later a neighbor told me that she had just discovered some moths in her house, and at this moment chills ran through my body, alerting me to take this as a warning sign. But I didn't; I pushed this feeling aside. I convinced myself that due to the fact that we've never had a moth problem before, there was no need to assume we had one now. A few more days had gone by when a teeny, tiny little moth flew up right to me in my room, as if it were looking me right in the face, forcing me to accept its existence. But I didn't; I pushed this feeling aside. I even said, "Look at that beautiful butterfly!" and went on my way. I seriously did not want to face reality at that point — so I didn't! If you don't look for something, you won't find it, right? Easy. That night, I dreamt about moths. And when I woke up early in the morning, the thought ran through my head over and over, it's time to check.

For whatever reason, that day I felt brave enough to look. I got out of bed, went over to my chest of drawers and opened it up to look through my clothes. I wasn't even sure what I was looking for. Were a bunch of little moths going to fly out? Would I just see all my sweaters eaten up? The clothes on top looked fine, and I had nearly convinced myself that I didn't need to look any further when in the corner of my eye, I saw something move.

There, in the bottom of my chest I saw a larva. A slimy, minuscule, tiny worm, creeping and crawling down the drawer, leading me to its siblings. And as I followed it down the path, I would find the beginning of the end.

Opening up my chest and finding these larvae felt like opening Pandora's box. Once you start looking, you can't stop. It was an undeniable infestation. They were everywhere. In our sweaters, our clothes, our suits, our blankets. On our guitar cases, suitcases, curtains, mattresses, sofa, and chairs. They were even on our walls and floors and ceiling. Hiding in the deep, dark cracks and corners, hidden from the naked eye. If there was a piece of fabric in our house, there were larvae on it. I always thought moths were only attracted to wool; I was wrong. I think wool is like ice cream to them. They love it, but if they are hungry enough, these little joy-sucking gremlins will munch through any, and I mean any thing.

It took three days to go through everything, three months to resolve, and years to replace all we had lost.

The process of solving a moth infestation takes time, assertive decision making, grace, and a whole lot of letting go. When moth larvae infest your belongings, there are three ways I've found work best to destroy the larvae and save the article: wash them out, freeze them out, or burn them out.

If something could be washed out, we tried that first.

But due to so many textiles not handling warm temperatures (they must be washed at least at sixty degrees Celsius or a hundred and forty Fahrenheit to kill off the pests), many things shrunk or were destroyed. Then we would try to freeze them out. Over the following months we'd stuff as much as we could into our tiny European freezer for a three-day cycle. The problem was that we were running against time. We could only fit so much in our freezer at once (and no, not too many people were keen on us bringing our moth-infested belongings to their house to put in their freezers), and the longer each cycle would wait its turn, the greater the chance that other items would be destroyed by the moths.

As a last resort, we tried burning things out. We'd put a few things at a time in the oven to bake and try to burn the larvae out. I might or might not have pulled out the fire extinguisher at three in the morning once, having forgotten to check on my wool socks that might or might not have gone up in flames.

When all these measures failed, we had to let go and throw things out for good. After this final stage of the process, we had lost so many of our belongings, it looked like we had been robbed; like a million little moth burglars came into our home and took with them as much as they could. It was intense and painful, and challenging to navigate, but it taught me one of the most valuable lessons of my life: how to decide when to keep something, and when to let it go.

With every article you pick up, you have to decide on a few things. Is this still worth the effort to save it? Do I have the capacity and tools to do so? Is this so far gone that I have to let it go?

Letting go of things in my life has never been comfortable or easy, whether it be physical, emotional, or relational. I'm not an extremely materialistic person, but I am a sentimental one. A lot of these treasures weren't just belongings, they were memories, part of my story. They were things that reminded me of someone I loved, or a time or place in my life that held an incredible experience. There were beautiful dresses my mother had bought me for my honeymoon, souvenirs from my trips to Ethiopia, anniversary presents from my wolf. Deciding what to keep and what to let go triggered a lot of pain in me, not so much from letting go of items, but from letting go of parts of my life.

As I picked up every article, deciding if it was worth trying to salvage, I began to reflect on the parts of my life at the time that I was also struggling to let go of. To put it frankly, my life was a mess. My (and my wolf's) work, community and relationships were all connected and were all in serious jeopardy. Unhealthy behaviors in people and structures were bringing about pain and destruction. People were getting hurt, systems were crumbling, work imploded and many people, like us, began to feel that the abuse was destroying more than we could salvage. But we didn't know how to handle it, or how to save it.

When your job, community and close friendships are all intertwined and entangled together, if just one of those areas begins to be affected by something unhealthy, one by one, all of them become affected. And if you don't stop, acknowledge there is a problem, resist 'possuming out', face the issues, and take an in-depth look at what's really going on, then, like in our home, it will spread and infest everything. And trust me, it did. My work, community, and relationships began to fall apart one by one.

So there I was, looking in my home and in my life, trying to decide what was salvageable. Is this still worth the effort to save it? Do I have the capacity and tools to do so? Is this so far gone that I have to let it go?

When you love someone or something very much, and abuse or dysfunctional behavior seeps into the relationship or the environment, it's very difficult to confront it. Much like I didn't want to address the moth infestation for fear of losing my belongings, I didn't want to confront my relationships or work environment either, for fear of losing them. It's the kind of fear that can make you blind to the harm something is causing you. You see the problems, but you fear that the absence of these precious things would bring more pain than just living with them. So you keep them. You'd rather keep that friendship, like wearing a sweater infested with larvae, than deal with it or let it go.

But people aren't 'things'. It's one matter to pick up an article of clothing and decide if you can part ways; it's another entirely when picking up a relationship to something or someone and doing the same. I found this process agonizing. I am a fighter. As I learned through my wolf, I believe in fighting for the things and dreams and people you love with everything you have. Unlike an opossum, I don't scare easily from adversity and I don't normally pull away from a relationship when there is turmoil or conflict. I stay and engage, and try my best to resolve the problems so we can continue our relationship in a healthy way. In order to do so, I knew I needed to actively fight for these things in the same way I fought for my belongings in my house: wash, freeze, burn, or let go.

If my relationship with a person was damaged, but possibly still salvageable, I first tried to wash it. I tried to wash out the filth and damage by approaching, dealing with and resolving the issues directly, purifying and making new. If this didn't work and no change was made, I froze it. I froze the relationship by putting it on pause, stepping away for a period of time, giving me (and maybe them) time to process and figure out a good approach to salvaging it. After some time, I took it out of the 'freezer', ready to try a new strategy. If I felt that I still couldn't deal with the damage done, I burned it. I let it die. I stopped interacting with it altogether. I stopped being its friend, stopped working for or with it, ignored it as if it was completely burnt out of my life. No time limit for when and if I would engage with it again. Truly letting it die. Sometimes we have to let things completely die in order for them to resurrect, and of course my hopes were that one day it would come back to me. And then, if all the washing and freezing and burning didn't work — only then, I felt ready to let it go for good. If felt as if I had done everything I could to save it and it was no longer capable of being saved. Only then could I completely let it go.

After days of dealing with the moths, I went to bed believing it was finished and the moths were gone. But as my head hit the pillow a sudden urge came over me that I had forgotten to check one spot. But where? I had cleaned top to bottom, left to right, every inch. I realized then that I had forgotten 'under'. I jumped out of bed and yelled to my wolf, "Under the rug!" as I ran into the living room to check my precious rug.

Oh, how I loved this beautiful, oriental, colorful rug that I had found on sale after years of eyeing it. I had coveted this rug. I designed my entire space around it, showed it off to everyone who came over to our home, and smiled every time I saw it. It was my treasure. That night, as I slowly bent down on my knees, turning my rug over, there, lying beneath all its beauty the larvae wriggled and squirmed. The infestation in my rug was so extreme that I knew no amount of washing, freezing or burning would salvage it; I had to let it go.

At this moment, after days of work, exhaustion, and decision making, I broke down and wept. I did not weep because of the rug, though that was a hard loss; I wept because I knew that, although there were many things and people that I treasured and loved and was forced to let go of, I could not begin to understand how it had gotten to this point and how I would even begin to move on.

The emptiness of my home reflected the emptiness I felt losing so many things and people. The fear of living without them hurt almost as badly as the pain they caused me. As I held my rug in my hands, which at that moment felt like a metaphor for my life, I cried out, "How can I let them go?" And at this moment, the lion in me whispered, "Sometimes we have to let things go while we still love them as treasures, before we hate them as predators."

Like no one wants to throw away their favorite rug, no one wants to throw away a friendship or a job they've invested in. But when you hold up that rug and realize it's no longer the favorite decoration it once was, it's the habitat of a larvae infestation, you know you need to let it go before it spreads to more of your house. So must you also know that once abuse or mistrust enters a relationship or a work environment, if it's not dealt with properly and immediately, it will only continue to spread pain, and turn quickly from something you once loved into something you now fear or hate. If it is unsalvageable, it's better to let go before it destroys you. As I braved looking under more of my rug, turning it over to discover the plethora of larvae, I began to ask myself the hardest question of all: how did this happen? How did so much destruction come in and how come it took so long to discover it?

Moths are attracted to deep, dark cracks of dirty, unkempt areas of your home that are neglected, mistreated and abandoned. There they lay their eggs and breed. After I had pruned so many things out of my space, I began to look deeper into the environment of my life that welcomed this infestation. Which areas of myself, my behavior and my character were so neglected and ignored that it became the perfect environment for so much destruction to breed?

When our lives start to fall apart, it's easy to believe that we are victims of wrongdoing — that when bad things happen to us, it's the fault of others and no responsibility of our own. Sometimes this is the case. Sometimes we are victims of the crimes of others and nothing we did or didn't do could change that. But when many different areas of our lives begin to fall apart, we need to look for a thread that connects them, and oftentimes it will lead back to us. Not necessarily because we caused it, but because we welcomed it.

In a matter of weeks, my wolf and I quit our jobs, let go of projects we had spent ten years running and said goodbye to over a dozen close friendships. We felt we had been mistreated, abused, mobbed, and manipulated by the environment and many of the relationships. And we were. People and leaders and friends we trusted let us down in astronomical ways. It was brutal, and it just about destroyed us, but somehow we knew we needed to move past this.

Although no one can take responsibility for anyone else's behavior or decisions, we can take responsibility for our own. It was very easy to sit in the anger and hurt and pain of what 'they' did to 'me'. Though it was painful and heartbreaking, the role of victim was not an identity that I or my wolf wanted to wear. We knew that if we remained there too long, then just like the larvae eating away at our belongings, piece by piece, so would the anger and pain eat away at us until we were broken beyond repair. If we didn't deal with the 'how', we knew it was only a matter of time before the 'when' would come back. When will this happen again?

So I dug deep into the cracks and crevices of myself, inspecting the areas in which I had neglected to set up boundaries with people, which in turn might have bred an environment where people took advantage of me. I inspected the areas where

I had 'possumed out' and didn't speak up when I initially saw something wrong, or felt hurt by something, which might have allowed others' poor and abusive behavior to grow. I learned more about the type of personality I have and which types of personalities oppose that, leading to more confrontation and pain. I learned which environments I work best in and which ones I should avoid. Then, after all the letting go and pruning ended, I inspected the part of me that was struggling to let go of my anger and resentment, which in the future could breed an environment that does not welcome healthy, good relationships. And then after I washed, froze, and burned out areas of myself, eventually letting them go, I mourned. Putting those belongings in over forty-two trash bags and taking them to the dumpster to be forever thrown away felt like putting my life in body bags and taking them to the morgue. It was so painful, letting go of so much trash in my life. Surprisingly, it was freeing, but it also felt lonely. I remember walking back into my empty home and asking my wolf, "How will we ever fill this place again?"

He said, "Maybe this isn't the place we are supposed to fill; maybe it's the place we needed to learn to let go, and a new place is where we can begin to refill."

Through this process, we realized that the environment we were in needed to change in order for us to see real change in our lives. We had also just discovered that the moths laid eggs under the floorboards of our home, and it would be impossible to treat them to the point that we could be sure this would never happen again. And by this point, emotionally, we had parted ways with so many things and people in our lives, we felt we needed a fresh start somewhere else. So we moved.

We packed up what was left of our belongings and our lives, and we moved. Slowly but surely, we rebuilt. We rebuilt our home, paying attention to anything that could be put out of sight or mind for so long that we would neglect it, not allowing the perfect environment for another infestation to develop. We did this in all the other areas of our lives as well. We rebuilt our work, relationships and community with new values, and a foundation for living in a way that was conducive to things that were healthy and not harmful. There were also relationships and projects which had been frozen or burnt out that we realized needed to come back into our lives. Instead of jumping back in head first, we allowed ourselves to heal and brought them back when we were ready. And the ones we didn't, we don't miss, because by letting them go we made room for new things.

This doesn't mean it was easy. Mourning the loss of things or people in our lives, and then trying to move forward building new ones, was one of the most painful seasons we've ever experienced. It didn't take weeks, or months. It took years. But it was one of the most necessary and most valuable seasons.

This season helped me understand how to live a life that is more aware of the damage things and people can cause, and how to actively and assertively handle them. It's impossible to build your life in a way that nothing bad can happen. If you do, you're not truly living, for living requires risk, and risk welcomes the possibility of hurt. Having relationships risks pain. Investing in dreams risks failure. Joining a community risks trouble. It's impossible to live without risk, but it's not impossible to risk and be aware of the environment you're actively participating in, and whether your actions are facilitating pain. And it's certainly not impossible to know when to salvage and when to let go, even when letting go might feel impossible.

THE PURSUIT OF LIGHT

Although it is well known that moths are attracted to artificial lights, the reason for this behavior is still a widely studied topic. One theory is transverse orientation, where moths maintain a fixed angle relative to a distant light source, such as the moon, for orientation — guiding them towards where they should go for survival needs such as food and mates. When exposed to modern, man-made lights such as light bulbs and flames, a moth's angle to the moon becomes altered. Attracted to and dazzled by the new light, moths stray from the moon's path and drift towards the new light, whose flames or power often lead to injury or death.

In November 1936, my grandfather, who at the time was a teenager living in a small Massachusetts town, made his first world journey with his two aunts around the globe. One of the mystical and mysterious lands they traveled to was China. Then and there, his passion and love for the Chinese people and culture began, and would soon pass down through our family's generations from him to his son, and from his son (my father) to me.

When my father was fifteen years old, his father's battle with polio led to his death when onset by pneumonia. His death was tragic and traumatizing for my young father. The grief tormented and haunted him throughout his life, shaping not only the man he would become, the decisions and choices he would make, but also the father he would be to my sister and me. He spent the rest of his life working through the anger and grief and achieving and atoning for a life he hoped his father would have been proud of.

Soon after my grandfather's death, my father went to college at Yale University, where he earned a degree in Mandarin — a degree that ended up being of no real professional use, as he eventually ended up working in advertising. But I believe he studied this language to connect and understand more of who his father was and why he loved Chinese culture.

Growing up, his love for China continued to weave throughout our home: the artwork on the walls, books, documents with my father's Chinese characters, and language skills that were always being practiced. And of course, the obligatory Thursday night Chinese restaurant visits where my father would practice his Mandarin to keep it 'sharp', as he would say. My father loved Chinese culture, and I loved that he loved it.

When I was twelve, my parents took a trip to China. It was a big deal for our family as it was the first time either one of my parents, especially my father, had traveled there. I remember being so excited for him to finally go and wondered what stories and souvenirs he would return with for us. A few weeks later, they returned with antiques, hand-painted puppets, jade bracelets, gorgeous artworks and silk fabrics. But the biggest treasure of all was the slideshow of pictures from their trip. That's right; it was the nineties, slides were where it was at.

As we scrolled through the photos, I was mesmerized by China's landscape, people and colors. I giggled at the pictures of my six foot three giant of a father walking among the crowded streets of Beijing, with his head standing out above the rest. I gasped at the grasshoppers eaten on sticks in the open market. I marveled at the beauty of the Yangtze River, the Great Wall, the Terracotta Army, Tiananmen Square, and all the incredible places my parents were privileged to see.

As we continued to go through the slides, I noticed in the background the parts of the photo that weren't the highlight of the guided tour. The hardship of the people, poverty, and many children alone on the streets. When I asked my father about the children, he told me, "Those are orphans." I didn't know what an orphan was and so I asked more questions. He proceeded to explain the orphan crisis in China and why there were so many children without parents. I'll never forget the pain I felt deep in my chest that night when trying to process as a young child the idea of not having a mother or father. I was so upset that I ran to my room and cried.

That night, for the first time, I heard what I believe to be my lion's voice. He said, "One day, you will adopt a little girl from China." Through the years, I held onto that promise like it was the biggest treasure of my life.

Like many, my relationship with my father was complicated and often difficult. The walls I believe that he built up around his heart when his father passed away often prevented me from finding a way into it. Of course, as a child, I didn't understand this complexity. I understood that I had a father who I desperately wanted to be close with, who often pushed me away for whatever reason. It felt as though no matter what I did to try and connect to him, make him proud of me, make him see me, it seemed never to be enough to get closer to him.

I'll never forget the day my parents divorced and my father left the house. I followed him outside to his car and watched him pack his bags and drive off. Though my feet felt frozen to the ground, my heart was chasing him down the road. I didn't want him to go. I never wanted him to go. But there he was, like the moon I'd been trying my whole life to get closer to, pulling farther and farther away from me.

For about a year after that, the contact between us became less and less. Phone calls rarely came in, and eventually, the Thursday night Chinese dinners stopped. The longing I had to connect and be closer to my father continued to disturb me. Without him, I felt lost and confused. Without his light, I had no idea where to go or what to do.

In hindsight, I believe this disorientation was a big part of why I packed my bags and left for Germany just a year or so later. I believe I thought that if I traveled around the world, went to places my father had been, to places he'd never been, it would bring me closer to him. My grandfather loved to travel and so did my father; maybe this would be our common legacy.

Over the years, I would send him postcards from wherever I went. I'd tell him about my adventures among tribal peoples in Ethiopia, riverboat trips along the Golden Triangle, motorcycle rides in India. But no place I visited ever excited him as much as my trips to China. Embracing all the incredible things that my father had shown me throughout my childhood, and finally being able to share those things meant everything to me. And over time, the travels did become a way for us to get closer. His enthusiasm grew, as well as our relationship, so I continued to travel and share with him all my adventures.

Years later, when my wolf and I were getting serious about marriage, I told him about that night back when I was going through my father's China slides, and I heard my lion tell me that I would adopt a little girl from China. He took that seriously and inherited the same dream for our family. I will never forget the moment of telling my father and seeing the excitement and pure joy it brought him when we started the adoption process. He helped us find the right Chinese characters for her name 柏贝 and began teaching me more about Chinese culture and how to raise her with it.

When we adopted Bo Bei in China, my father was so eager to meet her. I was so longing for her to meet her grandfather responsible for inspiring our love for her culture. We came back to our home in Germany with plans to go to the United States as soon as possible, excited for my father and the rest of my family to meet our daughter. Little did we know we would face unbelievable obstacles that prevented us from coming back as planned. We ran into unexpected legal threats from the German government regarding the legitimacy of our adoption (which we, later on, would prove in the courts was done entirely lawfully and legally). This fiasco prevented us from traveling until it was sorted out. During this time, the 2020 COVID pandemic broke out, and once again travels were banned. Suddenly six months passed, and we were still trapped in Germany, and my father still longed to meet our daughter. Over time, the illegitimate yet distressing threats from Germany increased. It became so stressful and traumatic that we, as a family, had to make the painful decision to leave Germany and move back to the United States.

I remember calling my father to tell him the news — that after fifteen years of living overseas, we were going to be moving back home. I didn't know how he would take it. I didn't know if he would be upset or disappointed. If he would call us failures or irresponsible. I didn't know if he would want me to come back. I didn't know if he wanted me. Shaking on the phone, I told him our plan. He was quiet, and then in the most tender voice, he said, "Finally, I get my daughter back."

Tears rolled down my face. After roaming around the world, trying to connect to my father, trying to make him proud, I realized that he, too, had longed all this time to connect to me and have me close. Perhaps all this time it wasn't about him pushing me away, but it was about him not knowing how to keep me close. How to be a father to me since he lost his father far too early in life. Now, the prodigal daughter was returning home into the welcoming arms of her father.

Immediately our family started to pack and prepare to come home. All we were waiting for was one last legal document from the courts allowing us to go. A few weeks later, when the documents were ready, we sent a text with a photo of the three of us standing in the courtroom to my father. He wrote back saying, 'The timing of this whole adventure is incredible. Give my granddaughter a hug from her Yéye.' Finally, we were legally free to go. After fifteen years of roaming around the world, searching for my moon, searching for home, searching for belonging, I finally felt free to come back home to my father and be with him.

The next morning, my sister called me to tell me that my father had unexpectedly passed away that evening from a heart attack.

The shock of my father's death felt like a moth that had been zapped by the false light it had mistaken all this time for the moon. I was trying so hard to connect to my father all these years, and once I finally decided to come back home and be near to him, I was zapped.

The theory is that moths orient themselves around the moon because they need it to guide them through life to survive.

Arguably, man-made lights distract and deviate them from that path. Like moths to moons, children look to their parents for guidance and direction on navigating through this world — how to survive and how to become who they are supposed to be. However, our parents are not meant to be our moons forever. When our parents' guidance and light turns into unachievable expectations set to gain approval and acceptance, our relationships can often turn unhealthy and even detrimental to our development.

Up until that moment on the phone, I believed my father was my moon, when all along, he was my lamp. Like my father did with his father, I spent far too much of my life desperately trying to get closer to my father's light, chasing and gravitating towards a man-made light whose construction was full of flaws. Wired and connected with parts that are extraordinary and parts that can easily be (and were) broken. A light that can turn off when it wants to. A light that was always meant to shine and radiate the amount of light it was capable of providing, but never meant to compare to the moon's eternal light. At some point we have to let go of our parents being our moons, and allow them to be our lamps.

For me personally, I have found that the only real moon and light that I want to follow is that which belongs to our maker, whom I believe to be God, the Heavenly Father, the wildest lion of all, whose light radiates from Him with love and strength. It is constant and trustworthy. It does not turn on or off depending on our behavior or efforts, but is everlasting. A light that shines with unconditional grace and pulls us close and shows us how to be a light in the darkness for others.

In Chinese folklore, legend has it that moths, especially the black ones, represent the spirits of the deceased. Some even believe that killing or disturbing a moth is considered taboo because it is likened to turning a former loved one away (clearly, I did not know this when I rid my house of moths a few years back!). Now when I see a moth, I like to believe it is a gentle reminder from my father to keep focused on the right lights in my life. To not be distracted by the false, shiny, artificial lights, but to stay focused on the moon. Focus on the lion I was created to be.

When I finally got back home to the United States and walked into my father's empty house, I found a small table with two chairs. On the table lay Chinese writing he had been sharpening up to practice with my daughter. There was a whole page devoted to her Chinese name and her characters. The second seat was for her.

I never met my father's father. And now, my daughter will never meet my father. That will haunt me for the rest of my life like a black moth. But my daughter will meet the moon. I will raise her to know the light that will guide her and pull her close to it no matter where she goes — teaching her how to live as a lion and find her own path, her own way. I will always be her lamp. I will always be available for her to turn to when she needs me and turn off when she doesn't. But I will not be her moon. I could never be her moon. Only the lion can be her moon.

THINGS I'VE LEARNED FROM MOTHS

- Trust your gut. If you feel something is 'off', respond to it immediately. It might be nothing, or it might be an infestation. Better safe than sorry (your clothes and relationships will thank you).

- Even though you don't want to look closely at things and face the issues, it doesn't mean they aren't real and that they will not have real consequences. Truth does not pause for ignorance. And problems, like larvae, don't magically disappear.

- Leaving things untouched and unseen for too long will not only bring neglect but harm. Things that are hidden away, backed into the darkest corners of our home, life and minds are targets for infestation, bringing damage, abuse, and pain. Your life is worth living in the light. Even the really scary, hard parts that you don't want to face. Even the ugly sweaters your aunt gave you for Christmas that you pack away and bring out only on the holidays when she comes. Bring them to the light. They are part of you; bring them forward and let them be seen. Or at least put them in a bag with a lot of lavender, OK? You can't fix everything or every relationship. So when necessary, let it die and trust for rebirth or something new.

- Your heart, like a freezer, can only take so much. Know its capacity. If it's too small for that big, infested rug, let it go before you break it.

- Not all that shimmers and shines is the light you're meant to follow.

You were created to follow the moon. Don't let the lamps in your life distract you. They can help you along your path but were never designed to guide you. Our need for others' approval is like a moth drifting toward a lamp. It seems beautiful but ultimately blinds us from the only approval and guide we were ever created to follow, the moon. Whether we are aiming to please, or even trying to escape others' influence, we must remember to not let their light lead us away from our true path in life.

"May the hunger of the moths that feed on the neglected and hidden prompt you to stay alert, keep to the path of light, and be on guard like a lion."

BECOMING A LION

Not only are they known throughout history as powerful and magical characters, lions are also animals that nearly all beasts of the wild respect, earning them the title, 'King of the Jungle'. They are predators and yet they are companions. They are wild, fierce, and dangerous, but they are also loyal, loving, playful animals. They thrive in their strengths and know when to depend on others when they are weak. They know who they are and where they belong, making these animals the ultimate symbol of my life, and why I am learning to 'become' a lion.

Through the lessons we've learned through the animals in this book, we have all along been learning to become lions. It might even surprise you to learn that lions have many of the characteristics found in these other animals. Like wolves, most lions live in socially organized packs, known as prides, ranging from just one pair to forty lions. Also like wolves, lions practice fighting one another inside the security and trust of their pride in order to prepare themselves for battle with their enemies and prey. Although lions are very loyal to their pride, some are banished to live like lone wolves, or even like the nomadic possums.

Possums, like lion babies, or cubs, live under the protection of their mothers until one day they go off on their own. Lions who are forced to live on their own either learn to defend themselves and live nomadically, never again belonging to one place or pride, or eventually go find a new pride to belong to. They might only become part of the new pride by proving their strength and dominance in battle with other lions. Though fighting is a huge part of a lion's life, they also believe rest and sleep are key to their survival. And unlike possums who play dead and fall into a comatose sleep, unresponsive to their enemies, lion prides are always on the alert, even in their sleep, much like bats.

We know that bats use their high sensitivity to be alert and aware of their surroundings at all times, just like lions who are always on guard. As the pride sleeps, male lions patrol their surroundings. And like bats, lions sleep during the day and do most of their hunting at night. They too have learned the benefits of the darkness and how to get the most out of it when they hunt. Unlike bats, lions have incredible night vision which they use to hunt their prey. Most hunting is done by females, and when they hunt they take their time, just like moths.

As moth larvae lay dormant until the conditions are right

to feed, and then do so quickly and ravenously, so do lions hunt and feed strategically and in the right conditions. Slowly and patiently they stalk their prey, and follow up with short bursts of speed and attacks. Moths have also taught us that when things are hidden away they can be neglected and weakened. So we can look to the lions who, in contrast, choose to live and hunt in open areas such as grasslands and savannahs. This environment helps them stay alert, on guard, and ready for battle at all times. However, this environment also leaves them open for attack, so just as a tortoise relies on its shell for cover, so does the lion depend on its powerful body that shields them in battle.

Lions have strong, compact bodies, lethal claws, teeth, and mighty forelegs. Like the tortoise's shell, a male lion's mane is its most recognizable feature. Although there is much debate about the purpose of the mane, including fitness, dominance, intimidation, and attracting mates, one argument has been to keep the neck and throat surrounded and make it difficult for predators to puncture. I like to think that, like a tortoise shell, it symbolizes great strength, power, and possibly protection. And as the cracks of a tortoise's shell represent the battles a tortoise has survived, it's been said that the length and color of a lion's mane can apparently signal the fighting success of the lion. A darker, fuller, longer mane can indicate a stronger and healthier animal. The more a lion has seen battle, the more he wears his scars like badges of pride for all to see and fear his strength.

I am not a lion. But I am striving every day to become one. To be strong and brave when faced with fear and danger. To rise above my shortcomings and to look past my insecurities, and look my enemies straight in the eyes with confidence. I am not a lion. But I am training every day to become one. Sharpening my dull claws, which have been worn down by the pain and brokenness of this world, with blades of grace and mercy until they are sharp enough to slash through my greatest fears. I am not a lion. But I am awakening the one inside me. The one who wants to rise above my anxieties, who wrestles with my shame, and who roars louder than the lies inside my head that daily tell me I am weak and not enough. I am not a lion, but I want to be. And I want to help you become a lion.

Learn to be a lion. Learning to become a lion is about knowing who you are and what you are called to do. It's understanding the power of your strengths and the vulnerability of your weaknesses, so that you may know what in this world you are meant to fight for and how to use your gifts and talents to do so. It's about knowing when to stand up to your enemies with bravery and might, and when to back down and rest.

Becoming a lion is about knowing and claiming your pack, confidently understanding your place inside it and why you belong to it. It's trusting others and allowing them to protect you and fight for you, while being trustworthy and reliable to fight for and protect others. It's being sharpened by your pack and strengthened by each other, and knowing when to stay in a pack and when to walk away. It's about being comfortable in seasons of solitude as well as seasons of community and family.

Becoming a lion is about daring to step outside your comfort zone and inherit the treasures of the dark, unknown seasons of your life. It's learning how to turn fears from things that once scared you back into things that spark your curiosity and bring you joy. It is being secure and empowered by your body and not imprisoned by its limitations. It's being proud of the parts of you that are broken, wearing them like scars that tell stories of the battles you've overcome, not ones that have overcome you. Becoming a lion is about becoming strong. Brave. Fierce and dangerous. I want to be a lion.

Surround yourself with lions. Surround yourself with people who are braver, stronger, sharper and fiercer than you. Be around people that mold, model, inspire and encourage you to become more like a lion. People who choose to see you in your fullest strengths, even when you're living in your lowest weaknesses. People who see your flaws, scrapes and bruises and love you not in spite of them, but because of them. People who help you take on the biggest giants in your life by knowing when to battle them alongside you, and when to support you in doing it alone. People who see you as a lion, even while you're still becoming one. Surround yourself with lions.

Help others become lions. At some point in our lives we have all felt broken, misplaced, nomadic and lost. We have been scared of the darkness and let the things we loved become the things we fear. We've confused confrontation with something to be avoided, and we've backed down from fighting for things we believe in because we're untrained and unprepared for battle. We've been forgotten by people we've loved and we've been loved by people we've forgotten. We've been hurt, cast aside, and left to wander around this world trying to figure out who we are, where we belong, and why we are here. All it takes is one lion to come alongside you and say, "I see a lion in you; rise up!" I hope that throughout this book you've come to see that we've all feared our bats, fought like wolves, hid like possums, bred like moths, and carried our burdens like tortoises. And through all our journeys, battles, triumphs and failures, together we've become more like lions. For in our weaknesses we find our strengths. In our failures, we find our triumphs. In our loneliness, we find our belonging. And in our loss, we find our roar.

EPILOGUE

Soon after I finished writing this book, our family moved to a small cabin in the woods outside Atlanta, Georgia. As we unpacked our boxes and sunk our feet and hearts into the land we now call home, we were pleasantly surprised to discover our new, wild neighbors.

We were first greeted by Dinkey, an opossum (named by our daughter) who lives in the abandoned burrows in our forest and comes out every night to say hello to the stars. Then there was a tortoise, who slowly pulled his beautifully cracked shell through the brush and trudged down to the creek while nodding his head at us as he journeyed onward.

A few weeks later, we sighted a pack of coyotes and learned they are actually mixed with about one third wolf. They commune in our woods, singing us lullabies at night as they howl to the moon — which shines so brightly it attracts the most beautiful moths we've ever seen. They dance for us each night outside our windows, which we keep shut so as not to distract them with our lights.

And every evening, as we say goodnight to our lovely forest friends and close our front door, we also wave to the little bat who hangs above it. We've appropriately named her 'Angst'- the German word for fear. She hangs as a guardian to ward off fear not welcome in this home.

As amazed as we were to find all the characters that I've dreamed of for years and now written about in my book — it was a beautiful reminder that dreamers dare to dream the stories they wish to live. But it's the lions who are brave enough to make those dreams reality.

ABOUT THE AUTHOR

Liz Mannchen is passionate about empowering people to become braver and stronger — like a Lion. Liz has traveled to over forty countries in pursuit of that dream. Using illustrations and music from her band Liz and the Lions, to share stories, she is passionate about championing people to live powerful lives. She is a certified animal-assisted therapist and has always been deeply curious about the human-animal bond and what we can learn from animals. Together with her Husband, she runs the brand "Live As Lions", a company designed to equip people with products and services to help them live wild and free.

Here, Liz has put all the stories from the stage, her albums, travels, and studies into a book. From near-death experiences to conquering major fears (like vampires!) to overcoming heartbreak and moth infestations, Liz openhandedly reveals her difficult learning experiences so that others might, too, find treasures among their struggles and battles and learn to rise above them. Learn more about Liz and the world of Live As Lions at www.liveaslions.com

www.ingramcontent.com/pod-product-compliance
Lightning Source LLC
Chambersburg PA
CBHW041723070526
44585CB00006B/135